BABY BRIGHTS

BABY BRIGHTS

30 COLORFUL CROCHET ACCESSORIES

KATHLEEN MCCAFFERTY

New York

An Imprint of Sterling Publishing
1166 Avenue of the Americas
New York, NY 10036

Text © 2015 by Kathleen McCafferty
Photography & Illustrations © 2015 by Lark Crafts, an imprint of Sterling Publishing Co., Inc.

Design by Merideth Harte
Photography by Carrie Hoge
Illustrations by Orrin Lundgren

ISBN 978-1-4547-0876-6

Distributed in Canada by Sterling Publishing
c/o Canadian Manda Group, 664 Annette Street
Toronto, Ontario, Canada M6S 2C8
Distributed in the United Kingdom by GMC Distribution Services
Castle Place, 166 High Street, Lewes, East Sussex, England BN7 1XU
Distributed in Australia by Capricorn Link (Australia) Pty. Ltd.
P.O. Box 704, Windsor, NSW 2756, Australia

For information about custom editions, special sales, and premium and corporate purchases,
please contact Sterling Special Sales at 800-805-5489 or specialsales@sterlingpublishing.com.

Manufactured in China

2 4 6 8 10 9 7 5 3 1

larkcrafts.com

For my mom, Eilish McCafferty,
the best knitter and crocheter
I know, and the best mom a
girl could have. Thank you for
inspiring me along my own
creative journey. I love you.

CONTENTS

INTRODUCTION

Captivated by textures, colors, shapes, and sounds, babies are curious explorers of the world. They experience their surroundings by looking and grabbing at whatever they can reach. Usually this means that they place whatever they've grabbed straight into their mouths. You could argue that if they've taken hold of one of the lovingly-made projects from this book, they're simply displaying excellent taste!

Baby Brights presents an exciting array of crochet clothing, toys, and accessories for babies with contemporary designs in beautiful, bright colors. Perfect for beginners, seasoned crocheters, and even general crafters, the collection of designer projects in *Baby Brights* includes items to wear, to use in the nursery, for play, and for travel. The projects, organized by type: Rattles & Teethers, Bath Time, Hats, Booties, Toys, Nursery, and Blankets, are all to make, use, and enjoy while your baby is young, and to cherish for a lifetime.

The book begins with basic crochet stitch instructions to get you going or refresh your memory, as well as fundamental information about tools, yarn, and gauge. As you'll discover, it takes just a few simple stitches to make most of the projects in this collection. Each project is rated by skill level, so you can start where you're comfortable and work your way up to stitching more advanced designs. And because they're mostly small, the projects work up quickly and easily.

I have selected the materials and projects with mothers and babies in mind. Everything is safe for babies to use and explore, beautiful enough to please the most discerning mom, and easy to keep clean.

I hope you have as much fun crocheting these projects as sweet little ones will have snuggling, cuddling, and playing with your vibrant gifts.

—Kathleen

PART 1

The Basics

Getting Started

One of the wonderful things about crochet is that all you need is a hook, some yarn, and some scissors to get started. Plus, making wee items for babies means you don't need a lot of yarn, unless you're making a blanket or something big.

TOOLS & MATERIALS

HOOKS

Aluminum, plastic, bamboo, or steel? How do you know what kind of crochet hook is right for you? It all boils down to personal preference, really, so experiment to get a feel for what you like. If you're just getting started, aluminum and plastic are common choices, easy on the wallet, and come in variety packs with different sizes.

Hooks come in a range of sizes with the smallest used for lacework and the largest used for chunkier, thick yarns. They're sized according to thickness, in either a number or letter system, depending on the brand. See the Crochet Hook Sizes Chart for more information on hook sizing.

SCISSORS

Small scissors are great for cutting and trimming ends and can be easily toted around for quick projects on the go.

YARN NEEDLES

Yarn needles help with weaving in loose ends to neatly finish your project. They're similar to embroidery needles, but are big enough to accommodate yarn and have a blunt tip.

TAPE MEASURE

Keep a tape measure handy to measure your gauge as you work.

YARNS

Each project in this book lists the yarn weight and gauge; if you have trouble finding the exact yarn used by the designer, you can always use a substitute. Take a look at the Yarn Weight and Crochet Hook Standard Sizes Charts from the Craft Yarn Council to assist with any yarn substitutions you make.

SYNTHETICS

Acrylic, nylon, and polyester are all made from synthetic fibers. Yarns made from 100% synthetic fibers are a great choice for beginners, and can help you practice your technique before committing to more expensive yarn. Synthetics are also easily cared for and can be tossed in the wash, something important to consider when you've got a little one sticking things in their mouth at all times.

NATURAL FIBERS

Natural fibers are made from plant or animal fibers. Plant fiber yarns include cotton, bamboo, linen, hemp, and others. Yarns made from animal fibers include mohair, cashmere, alpaca, and wool. Each fiber stitches up a little differently and has its own unique set of properties. I recommend that you stick to the type of yarn fiber listed for each project in this book for the best result, although you can certainly experiment if you wish.

STANDARD YARN WEIGHT CHART

Yarn Weight Symbol and Category Names	**0** LACE	**1** SUPER FINE	**2** FINE	**3** LIGHT	**4** MEDIUM	**5** BULKY	**6** SUPER BULKY
Types of Yarns in Category	Fingering 10-count crochet thread	Sock, Fingering, Baby	Sport, Baby	DK, Light Worsted	Worsted, Afghan, Aran	Chunky, Craft, Rug	Bulky, Roving
Crochet Gauge* Ranges in Single Crochet to 4 inches	32–42 double crochets**	21–32 sts	16–20 sts	12–17 sts	11–14 sts	8–11 sts	5–9 sts
Recommended Hook in Metric Size Range	Steel*** 1.6–1.4 mm	2.25–3.5 mm	3.5–4.5 mm	4.5–5.5 mm	5.5–6.5 mm	6.5–9 mm	9 mm and larger
Recommended Hook U.S. Size Range	Steel*** 6, 7, 8 Regular hook B–1	B–1 to E–4	E–4 to 7	7 to I–9	I–9 to K–10 1/2	K–10 1/2 to M–13	M–13 and larger

* Guidelines only: The above reflect the most commonly used gauges and needle or hook sizes for specific yarn categories.

** Lace weight yarns are usually knitted or crocheted on larger needles and hooks to create lacy, openwork patterns. Accordingly, a gauge range is difficult to determine. Always follow the gauge stated in your pattern.

*** Steel crochet hooks are sized differently from regular hooks—the higher the number, the smaller the hook, which is the reverse of regular hook sizing.

CROCHET HOOK SIZES CHART

MILLIMETER RANGE	U.S. SIZE RANGE*	MILLIMETER RANGE	U.S. SIZE RANGE*
2.25 mm	B–1	6 mm	J1–0
2.75 mm	C–2	6.5 mm	K–10 1/2
3.25 mm	D–3	8 mm	L–11
3.5 mm	E–4	9 mm	M/N–13
3.75 mm	F–5	10 mm	N/P–15
4 mm	G–6	15 mm	P/Q
4.5 mm	7	16 mm	Q
5 mm	H–8	19 mm	S
5.5 mm	I–9		

* Letter or number may vary. Rely on the millimeter (mm) sizing.

Stitches & Techniques

MAKING THE FIRST LOOP

Every crochet stitch starts and ends with one loop on the hook. All crochet is made from a series of loops, and the first loop begins as a slip knot, which doesn't count as your first stitch.

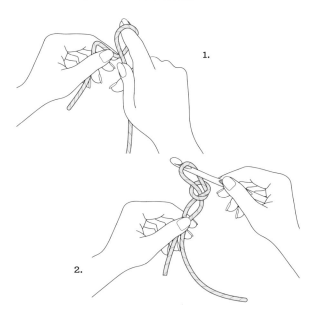

1.

2.

To make a slip knot, hold the yarn between the thumb and middle finger of your left hand with the tail falling down. Wrap the yarn over the top and behind the index finger ①. Wrap again over the index finger and pull a loop of yarn through the middle of the circle on your hand. While pulling this loop up with the hook in right hand and holding the tail with your left hand, slip the circle off your fingers ②. Tighten by pulling the tail. Make your loop smaller to fit your hook by gently pulling the yarn coming from the skein, but don't make it too tight—you need to be able to work a stitch into it.

YARN OVER (YO)

Yarn over is when you wrap the yarn over your crochet hook from back to front. See illustration in Chain Stitch. You yarn over in every crochet stitch either before or after inserting your hook into the next stitch. Some stitches require yarning over two or more times. Trying to yarn over from front to back will cause your stitches to become tangled and twisted.

CHAIN STITCH (CH)

The chain stitch is the starting point for most crochet projects, and is used to make the first row or round of your project. To make a chain stitch, start with your slip knot snugly on the hook, then yarn over (yo) and pull the yarn through the loop on the hook. That's your first chain. Continue in this way until you reach the desired number of stitches. Keep a relaxed grip on your yarn as you work, and don't make your chain stitch too tight or you'll find it difficult to work stitches into it as you move forward.

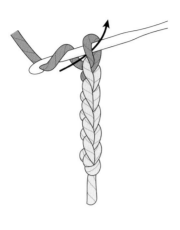

SINGLE CROCHET (SC)

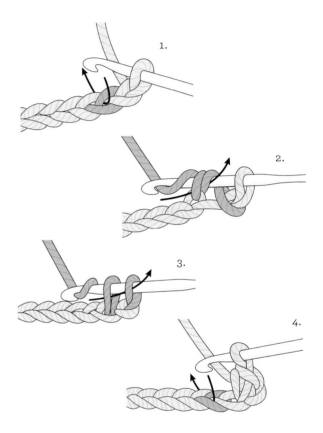

SLIP STITCH (SL ST)

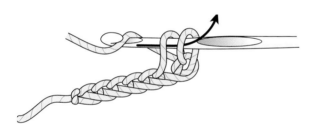

The slip stitch is the shortest of the crochet stitches and is often used for piecing squares together or stitching sides. To make a slip stitch, insert your hook into the next stitch and yarn over (yo) and pull back through the stitch and the loop on the back.

The single crochet stitch (sc) is the foundation of crochet. Once you master this basic stitch, you're set, as most crochet stitches are a variation of this stitch. To make a single crochet, insert your hook into the stitch ①. Yarn over (yo) and pull back through the stitch ②. Then yarn over and pull the yarn through both loops on the hook ③. Insert your hook into the next stitch to begin again ④.

HALF DOUBLE CROCHET (HDC)

DOUBLE CROCHET (DC)

The half double crochet stitch (hdc) works up fast and is a common stitch for making hats, garments, and other accessories. To make a half double crochet stitch, yarn over (yo) and insert the hook into the stitch ①, yarn over and pull back through the stitch, creating three loops on the hook ②. Yarn over and pull the yarn through all three loops on the hook ③, with one loop remaining on the hook ④.

Double crochet is like the half double crochet stitch in that you yarn over (yo) before inserting your hook into the next stitch. To make a double crochet stitch, yarn over once and insert your hook into the next stitch ①. Then yarn over and draw the yarn through the stitch, creating three loops on the hook ②. Yarn over and pull the yarn through two loops on the hook ③, yarn over again and pull the yarn through the remaining two loops on the hook ④. Yarn over and insert your hook into the next stitch to begin again ⑤.

TREBLE CROCHET (TR)

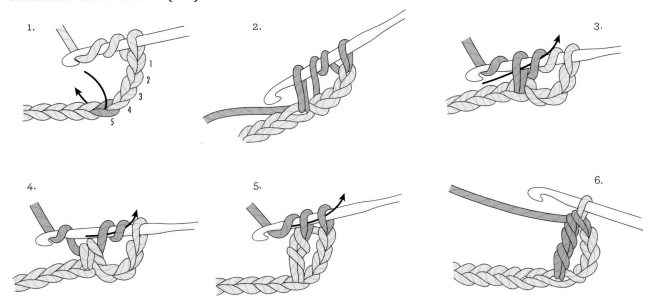

Treble crochet is a tall stitch that's also referred to as the triple crochet. It creates an open, airy fabric with more drape than the single or half double crochet stitches. To make a treble crochet, yarn over (yo) twice and insert your hook into the next stitch ①. Yarn over and pull the yarn back through the stitch, creating four loops on the hook ②. Yarn over and pull the yarn through the first two loops on the hook ③. You should now have three loops on your hook. Yarn over and pull the yarn through the next two loops on the hook ④. You should have two loops remaining on your hook. Yarn over and pull the yarn through both loops on the hook ⑤. The finished stitch is pictured in step ⑥.

DOUBLE CROCHET 2 TOGETHER (DC2TOG)

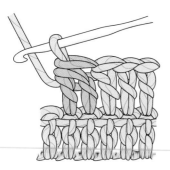

Also known as double crochet decrease, this stitch enables you to make your work smaller in certain areas, for shape. To make a double crochet 2 together, yarn over (yo) and insert your hook into the stitch. Yarn over and draw the yarn back through the stitch, yarn over and pull through the first two loops on the hook, leaving two loops remaining on the hook. Yarn over and insert your hook into the next stitch. Yarn over and pull the yarn back through the stitch. Yarn over and pull the yarn through the first two loops on the hook, then yarn over and pull through the remaining three loops on the hook.

WORKING IN THE ROUND

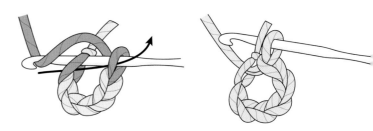

For the hats, booties, washcloths, and rugs in this book, you'll be working in the round. To work in the round, stitch the desired number of chains and then join the last chain with the first to form a ring. This is the foundation for your project, and from here you'll work your stitches into the previous round.

FASTENING OFF

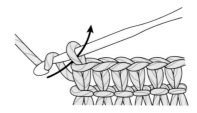

You're ready to fasten off when you've completed the last row or round of your project. To fasten off, cut the yarn, leaving a 4-inch-long (10 cm) tail, and pull it through the last loop on the hook to secure a knot.

BLOCKING

Blocking helps shape your pieces and makes your stitches look neat and uniform. To block, fill a sink with lukewarm water and dip your piece into the bath. You can also use a spray bottle and spritz the piece you want to block. Gently squeeze the water out and pin it with rustproof pins on a flat surface, like a corkboard or ironing board covered by a thick towel. Use your fingers to shape and pin the piece to the desired effect. Allow the piece to dry completely before removing the pins.

JOINING SEAMS

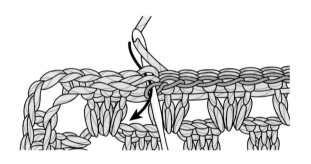

Unless otherwise stated in the projects, you can join items together using the slip stitch method. To create this seam, place pieces with right sides facing and align the stitches to match up on each side. Join with a slip stitch by inserting the hook in the back loop of the stitch on the piece closest to you and into the front loop of the stitch of the piece farthest from you. Keep working the slip stitches into the sides in this way. For a less bulky seam, you can also thread a yarn needle and seam the pieces together using a basic whipstitch.

WEAVING ENDS

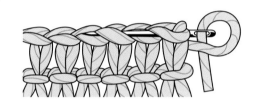

Weave in loose threads, such as the tail, by using a yarn needle and inserting the needle into neighboring stitches. By weaving the yarn through the stitches, you can hide and encase the ends to prevent fraying or separating down the road.

Abbreviations Used in Patterns

(this does not include special stitches defined within individual patterns)

- **approx** = approximately
- **beg** = begin(ning)(s)
- **BL** = back loop(s)
- **ch** = chain
- **ch-sp** = chain space previously made
- **cm** = centimeter(s)
- **dc** = double crochet
- **dc2tog** = double crochet 2 together
- **dc3tog** = double crochet 3 together
- **g** = gram(s)
- **hdc** = half double crochet
- **hdc2tog** = half double crochet 2 together
- **m** = meter(s)
- **mm** = millimeter(s)
- **oz** = ounce(s)
- **rem** = remain(ing)
- **rep** = repeat(s)
- **rnd(s)** = round(s)
- **RS** = right side
- **rsc** = reverse single crochet
- **sc** = single crochet
- **sc2tog** = single crochet 2 together
- **sc3tog** = single crochet 3 together
- **sk** = skip
- **sl st** = slip stitch
- **sp(s)** = space(s)
- **st(s)** = stitch(es)
- **tr** = treble crochet
- **yd** = yard(s)
- **WS** = wrong side

PART 2

The Projects

Apple Tree Rattles

Design by Annemarie Haakblog

Skill Level: Easy
Finished Measurements:
Height 3 inches/7.5 cm
Circumference 6 inches/15 cm (at widest)

Materials & Tools:
Schachenmayr Catania (100% cotton;
1.75 ounce/50 g = 137 yards/125 m)
and Phildar Coton 3 (100% cotton; 1.75
ounce/50 g = 132 yards/121 m): small
amounts each of (A), color dark brown;
(B), color dark green; (C), color light
green; (D), color orange; (E), color red;
(F), color mustard; (G), color turquoise;
(H), color rust—approx 1056 yards/968 m
of double-knit weight yarn
Note: You will not need a whole ball of
each color.

• **Crochet hook:** 2.75 mm (size C-2 U.S.)
• Fiberfill stuffing
• Small jingle bell (optional)
• Yarn needle

Gauge: Gauge is not critical for this
project.

Stitches:
chain (ch)
single crochet (sc)
slip stitch (sl st)
half double crochet (hdc)
single crochet 2 together (sc2tog)

Notes:

1. Gauge is not critical for this project, but work tightly so that stuffing will not show through stitches and rattle is sturdy.
2. All parts of rattle can be made with any color desired.
3. The treetop begins with an adjustable ring. If preferred, you can begin by working a ch 2 and working the first round of stitches into the 2nd ch from hook.
4. Change color when instructed and as desired to make stripes on treetop.

5. To change color, work last stitch of old color to last yarn over. Yarn over with new color and draw through all loops on hook to complete stitch. Proceed with new color. Fasten off old color, leaving a long tail to weave in and hide inside rattle.

INSTRUCTIONS

TREETOP:

With treetop color of your choice, make an adjustable ring.

Rnd 1 (RS): Work 8 sc in ring; join with sl st in first sc—8 sc.

Rnd 2: Ch 2 (does not count as a st), 2 hdc in each sc around; join with sl st in first hdc—16 hdc.

Rnd 3: Ch 2, 2 hdc in each hdc around; join with sl st in first hdc—32 hdc.

Rnds 4–8: Ch 2, hdc in each hdc around; join with sl st in first hdc.

Rnd 9: Ch 1, *sc2tog; rep from * around; join with sl st in first sc—16 sc.

Rnd 10: Ch 1, sc in each st around; join with sl st in first sc.

If RS of stitches are facing inside treetop, turn treetop inside out. Fill treetop with fiberfill. If desired, wrap a small jingle bell inside the fiberfill before inserting in treetop to make a rattle.

Rnd 11: Ch 1, sc in each st around; join with sl st in first sc.

Rnd 12: Ch 1, *sc2tog; rep from * around; join with sl st in first sc—8 sc. Fasten off.

TREE TRUNK:

Rnd 13: With RS facing, draw up a loop of trunk color of your choice in the joining sl st of the previous rnd, ch 1, sc in each sc around; join with sl st in first sc.

Rnds 14-20: Ch 1, sc in each sc around; join with sl st in first sc.

Fill trunk with fiberfill.

Rnd 21: Ch 1, *2 sc in next sc, sc in next sc; join with sl st in first sc—12 sc.

Rnd 22: Ch 1, sc in each sc around; join with sl st in first sc.

Rnd 23: Ch 1, working in back loops only, sc in each st around; join with sl st in first sc. Fasten off leaving a long tail. Add a little more fiberfill if needed. Weave tail through stitches of the last round and pull to close opening. Weave in end securely.

APPLES:

Make as many apples as desired.

With apple color of your choice, ch 2.

Row 1: Work 4 sc in 2nd ch from hook, do not join into a round.

Fasten off, leaving a long tail.

FINISHING:

Tie the apples to the tree using the long tail on the apples. Pull a length of cotton (color of your choice) through the middle of each apple for a tiny branch; tie a tight knot and trim ends. Weave in any remaining ends.

Fish Rattles

Design by Kristen Leitner

Skill Level: Easy
Finished Measurements:
Approximately 7 inches/18 cm long, 2½ inches/6.5 cm wide, and 2½ inches/6.5 cm tall

Materials & Tools:
Knit Picks Wool of the Andes (100% Peruvian highland wool; 1.75 ounces/50 g = 110 yards/101 m): (A), 1 ball, light color of your choice; (B), 1 ball, contrasting color of your choice; (C), small amount of black to embroider face—approx 220 yards/202 m worsted weight yarn
Note: You will not need a whole ball of every color.

- Crochet hook: 3.75mm (size F-5 U.S.)
- Stitch marker
- Yarn needle
- Wool stuffing
- Plastic rattle disk

Gauge: Gauge is not critical for this project.

Stitches:
chain (ch)
single crochet (sc)
single crochet 2 together (sc2tog)

Notes:

1. To change color, work last stitch of old color to last yarn over. Yarn over with new color and draw through all loops on hook to complete stitch. Proceed with new color, do not fasten off old color until instructed to do so. Carefully carry color not in use up inside of fish when next needed.
2. Gauge is not critical for this project. Work tightly to ensure that the stuffing does not show through the stitches.

INSTRUCTIONS

FISH BODY:

Beg at center of face, with A, ch 2.

Rnd 1: Work 6 sc in 2nd ch from hook—6 sts. Place a marker in last sc to indicate end of round. Move marker up as each round is completed. The joining seam runs along the bottom of the fish.

Rnd 2: Work 2 sc in each sc around—12 sts.

Rnd 3: *Sc in next sc, 2 sc in next sc; rep from * around—18 sts.

Rnd 4: *Sc in next 2 sc, 2 sc in next sc; rep from * around—24 sts.

Rnd 5: *Sc in next 3 sc, 2 sc in next sc; rep from * around—30 sts.

Rnd 6: *Sc in next 4 sc, 2 sc in next sc; rep from * around—36 sts.

Rnd 7: *Sc in next 5 sc, 2 sc in next sc; rep from * around; change to B in last st—42 sts.

Begin Body Striping:

Rnds 8 and 9: With B, sc in each sc around; change to A in last st.

Rnd 10: With A, sc in each sc around.

Rnd 11: With A, [sc in next 7 sc, sc2tog] 4 times, sc in last 6 sc; change to B in last st—38 sts.

Embroider Face: With yarn needle and C, use Back Stitch to embroider smile. Be sure to work from the wrong side of the circle of solid A that you have already crocheted. Be careful to position the middle of the smile lined up with the stitch marker (so the seam will remain on the bottom of the fish). After embroidering, knot the ends of the yarn together on the inside of the piece and trim excess. Working from WS with C, embroider two French Knots above smile for eyes. Knot ends together securely and trim excess.

Rnds 12 and 13: With B, sc in each sc around; change to A in last st.

Rnd 14: With A, sc in each sc around.

Rnd 15: With A, [sc in next 7 sc, sc2tog] 4 times, sc in last 2 sc; change to B in last st—34 sts.

Rnds 16 and 17: With B, sc in each sc around; change to A in last st.

Place small amount of wool stuffing in fish. Wrap plastic rattle disk with thin layer of wool stuffing and insert in fish, ensuring that it is flat behind the face of the fish. Continue to stuff the fish as you work.

Rnd 18: With A, sc in each sc around.

Rnd 19: With A, [sc in next 6 sc, sc2tog] 4 times, sc in last 2 sc; change to B in last st—30 sts.

Rnds 20 and 21: With B, sc in each sc around; change to A in last st.

Rnd 22: With A, sc in each sc around.

Rnd 23: With A, *sc in next 4 sc, sc2tog; rep from * around; change to B in last st—25 sts.

Rnd 24: With B, sc in each sc around.

Rnd 25: With B, *sc in next 3 sc, sc2tog; rep from * around; change to A in last st—20 sts.

Rnd 26: With A, sc in each sc around.
Rnd 27: With A, *sc in next 3 sc, sc2tog; rep from * around; change to B in last st—16 sts.
Rnd 28: With B, sc in each sc around.
Rnd 29: With B, [sc in next 3 sc, sc2tog] 3 times, sc in last sc; change to A in last st—13 sts.
Rnd 30: With A, sc in each sc around.
Rnd 31: With A, [sc in next 3 sc, sc2tog] twice, sc in last 3 sts; change to B in last st—11 sts.
Rnd 32: With B, sc in each sc around.
Fasten off both A and B, leaving long tails. With yarn needle, pull threads inside fish and knot securely. Trim excess.

FINS (MAKE 2):
With B, ch 2.
Rnd 1: Work 4 sc in 2nd ch from hook—4 sts. Place a marker in last sc to indicate end of round. Move marker up as each round is completed.
Rnd 2: Work 2 sc in each sc around—8 sts.
Rnd 3: *Sc in next sc, 2 sc in next sc; rep from * around—12 sts.
Rnd 4: *Sc in next 2 sc, 2 sc in next sc; rep from * around—16 sts.
Rnd 5: *Sc in next 3 sc, 2 sc in next sc; rep from * around—20 sts.
Rnd 6: *Sc in next 4 sc, 2 sc in next sc; rep from * around—24 sts.
Rnds 7 and 8: Sc in each sc around.
Rnd 9: *Sc in next 4 sc, sc2tog; rep from * around—20 sts.
Rnd 10: *Sc in next 3 sc, sc2tog; rep from * around—16 sts.
Stuff fin with wool.

Rnd 11: *Sc in next 2 sc, sc2tog; rep from * around—12 sts.
Rnd 12: Sc2tog around—6 sts.
Rnd 13: [Sc2tog] 3 times—5 sts.
Fasten off, leaving a long tail.

FINISHING:
Using the long tail, sew the fins to the rear of the fish, one on top of the other. Pull tails through the bottom of the fish, and knot firmly. Trim excess and push ends to the inside of the fish.

Heart Rattles

Design by Rosemary Newman

Skill Level: Easy

Finished Measurements:
Height 4 inches/10 cm

Materials and Tools:
Red Heart Kids Yarn (100% acrylic;
5 ounces/141 g = 290 yards/265 m):
2 different colors of your choice—approx
580 yards/530 m worsted weight yarn
Note: You will not need a whole ball
of each color.

• Crochet hook: 3.25 mm (size D-3 U.S.)
• Yarn needle
• Stitch marker
• Polyester stuffing
• Flat rattle disk insert, 1¼–1½ inches/
  33–38 mm diameter

Gauge: Gauge is not critical for this
project.

Stitches:
chain (ch)
slip stitch (sl st)
single crochet (sc)
single crochet 2 together (sc2tog)

Notes:

1. Each rattle is made from three pieces: two heart cups for top of rattle and one body. The heart cups are made first and then sewn together, side by side. The body is then started by working into the remaining (unsewn) stitches of the joined heart cups.
2. Cups and body are worked using different colors of your choice.
3. Pieces are crocheted in continuous spirals.
4. Gauge is not critical for this project. A small hook is used to ensure that the stitches are worked tightly and the stuffing does not show through the stitches.

INSTRUCTIONS

HEART CUPS (MAKE 2):

With cup color, ch 3; join with sl st in first ch to form a ring.

Rnd 1: Ch 2 (counts as first sc), work 5 sc in ring, sc in 2nd ch of beg ch-2—6 sc. Place a marker in last sc to indicate end of round. Move marker up as each round is completed.

Rnd 2: Work 2 sc in each st around—12 sc.

Rnd 3: [Sc in next st, 2 sc in next st] 6 times—18 sc.

Rnds 4–8: Sc in each st around.

Fasten off.

JOINING CUPS:

Hold heart cups together side by side and with open ends up. With yarn needle and short length of yarn, sew side edges together across two stitches.

BODY:

Rnd 1 (RS): Hold heart cups with opened ends up; join body color with sl st in edge of seam between cups, ch 1, sc in each st around, sc in beg ch-1—35 sc. Place a marker in last sc to indicate end of round. Move marker up as each round is completed.

Rnd 2: Sc in each st around.

Rnd 3: *Sc in next 5 sts, sc2tog; rep from * around—30 sc.

Rnd 4: Sc in each st around.

Rnd 5: *Sc in next 4 sts, sc2tog; rep from * around—25 sc.

Rnd 6: Sc in each st around.

Rnd 7: *Sc in next 3 sts, sc2tog; rep from * around—20 sc.

Rnd 8: Sc in each st around.

Loosen loop on hook and remove hook. Insert stuffing into heart cups, add rattle insert and continue stuffing as opening gets smaller. Insert hook back into loop, tighten loop and continue crocheting.

Rnd 9: *Sc in next 2 sts, sc2tog; rep from * around—15 sc.

Rnd 10: Sc in each st around.

Rnd 11: *Sc in next st, sc2tog; rep from * around—10 sc.

Rnd 12: [Sc2tog] 5 times—5 sc.

Fasten off.

FINISHING

Weave in any remaining ends.

Jingle Ball Rattles

Design by Rosemary Newman

Skill Level: Easy

Finished Measurements:
Height 4 inches/10 cm

Materials & Tools:
Red Heart Kids Yarn (100% acrylic;
5 ounces/141 g = 290 yards/265 m):
9 different colors of your choice—
approx 2610 yards/2385 m worsted
weight yarn
Note: You will not need a whole ball of
every color.

- Crochet hook: 3.25 mm (size D-3 U.S.)
- Yarn needle
- Stitch marker
- Polyester stuffing
- Ball rattle disk insert, 1½–1½ inches/
  35–38 mm diameter

Gauge: Gauge is not critical for this
project.

Stitches:
chain (ch)
slip stitch (sl st)
single crochet (sc)
single crochet 2 together (sc2tog)

Notes:

1. Pieces are crocheted in continuous spirals.
2. The instructions are for a nine-color ball, with color changed every 2 rounds.
3. To change color, work last stitch of old color to last yarn over. Yarn over with new color and draw through all loops on hook to complete stitch. Fasten off old color. Hide and secure yarn tails inside the ball as you work.
4. Gauge is not critical for this project. A small hook is used to ensure that the stitches are worked tightly and the stuffing does not show through the stitches.

INSTRUCTIONS

With first color, ch 3; join with sl st in first ch to form a ring.

Rnd 1: Ch 2 (counts as first sc), work 5 sc in ring, sc in 2nd ch of beg ch-2—6 sc. Place a marker in last sc to indicate end of round. Move marker up as each round is completed.

Rnd 2: Work 2 sc in each st around—12 sc.

Rnd 3: [Sc in next st, 2 sc in next st] 6 times; change to 2nd color in last st—18 sc.

Rnd 4: With 2nd color, *sc in next st, 2 sc in next st; rep from * around—27 sc.

Rnd 5: *Sc in next 2 sts, 2 sc in next st; rep from * around; change to 3rd color in last st—36 sc.

Rnds 6 and 7: With 3rd color, sc in each st around; change to 4th color in last st of rnd 7.

Rnd 8: With 4th color, *sc in next 3 sts, 2 sc in next st; rep from * around—45 sc.

Rnd 9: Sc in each st around; change to 5th color in last st.

Rnds 10 and 11: With 5th color, sc in each st around; change to 6th color in last st of rnd 11.

Rnd 12: With 6th color, sc in each st around.

Rnd 13: *Sc in next 3 sts, sc2tog; rep from * around; change to 7th color in last st—36 sc.

Rnds 14 and 15: With 7th color, sc in each st around; change to 8th color in last st of rnd 15. Loosen loop on hook and remove hook. Insert stuffing into lower half of ball, add rattle insert and continue stuffing as opening gets smaller. Insert hook back into loop, tighten loop and continue crocheting.

Rnd 16: With 8th color, *sc in next 2 sts, sc2tog; rep from * around—27 sc.

Rnd 17: *Sc in next st, sc2tog; rep from * around; change to 9th color in last st—18 sc.

Rnd 18: With 9th color, *sc in next st, sc2tog; rep from * around—12 sc.

Rnd 19: *Sc2tog; rep from * around—6 sc. Fasten off.

FINISHING:

Weave in any remaining ends.

Rainbow Teething Keys

Design by Rebekah Desloge

Skill Level: Easy

Finished Measurements:
Height 6 inches/15 cm

Materials & Tools:
T-shirt yarn (cotton and polyester blend with more cotton than polyester): (A), hot pink; (B), neon orange; (C), neon yellow; (D), neon green; (E), electric blue; (F), bold purple; (G), coral

- Crochet hook: 6 mm (size J-10 U.S.) or size to obtain gauge
- Tapestry needle

Gauge:
12 sts and 5 rows = 5 inches/13 cm.
Always take time to check your gauge.

Stitches:
chain (ch)
slip stitch (sl st)
single crochet (sc)

INSTRUCTIONS

MAKING T-SHIRT YARN:
Fold T-shirt in half lengthwise leaving about 1 inch/ 2.5 cm uncovered on the side edge.
Cut off the hem.
Cut 1 inch/ 2.5cm strips across the T-shirt, but not through the uncovered edge.
Once you reach the sleeve of the T-shirt, cut all the way across the T-shirt.
Open up the section of T-shirt with strips, and cut the uncut edge on the diagonal to join the strips.
Stretch the yarn as you wind it into a ball.

KEYS:
Disks (make 6—one each with A, B, C, D, E, and F):
Ch 4; join with sl st in first ch to form a ring.
Rnd 1: Ch 1, 5 sc in ring; join with sl st in beg ch-1—5 sc.
Rnd 2: Ch 1, 2 sc in each sc around; join with sl st in beg ch-1—10 sc.
Rnd 3: Ch 1, 2 sc in each sc around; join with sl st in beg ch-1—20 sc.
Sl st in next sc (first sc of rnd 3). Fasten off.

RING:
With G, ch 20.
Arrange disks in preferred color order and thread onto the G-colored chain; join G-colored chain with sl st in first ch to form a large G-colored ring.
Next rnd: Ch 1, work 25 sc evenly spaced into the G-colored ring, moving the disks around as needed to keep them out of the way as you work; join with sl st in first sc. Fasten off.

FINISHING: Weave in ends.

Teething Rings

Design by Sarah Bain

Skill Level: Easy

Finished Measurements:
Crochet fabric is about 2 inches/5 cm long and about 4¾ inches/11.5 cm wide, unstretched and before attaching to teether ring.

Materials & Tools:
Lily Sugar n' Cream (100% cotton; 2.5 ounces/71 g = 120 yards/109 m): about 7 yards/6.5 m for each teether, color of your choice—approx 7 yards/6.5 m worsted weight yarn

- Crochet hook: 4 mm (size G-6 U.S.) or size to obtain gauge
- Yarn needle
- Wooden teether rings, 3-inch/7.5 cm ring ½ inch/1.5 cm thick

Gauge:
12 sc = 4 inches/10 cm and 3 rows = 1 inch/2.5 cm
Always take time to check your gauge.

Stitches:
chain (ch)
single crochet (sc)
slip stitch (sl st)

INSTRUCTIONS

Ch 14.

Row 1: Sc in 2nd ch from hook and in each ch across—13 sc.

Rows 2–5: Ch 1, turn, sc in each sc across.

Joining Row: Wrap piece around wooden ring, matching sts of last row with chains at base of sts of first row; working through both thicknesses, sl st in each st across to secure to ring.
Fasten off.

FINISHING:
Weave in ends.

Bear Wash Mitts

Design by Clare Trowbridge

Skill Level: Beginner

Finished Measurements:
Diameter 4 inches/10 cm

Materials & Tools:
Twilley's of Stamford Freedom Sincere
(100% organic cotton; 1.75 ounces/50 g
= 126 yards/115 m): (A), 1 ball, color silver
fern #610 OR color sand #601 OR color
ocean #608—approx 126 yards/115 m of
double-knit weight yarn 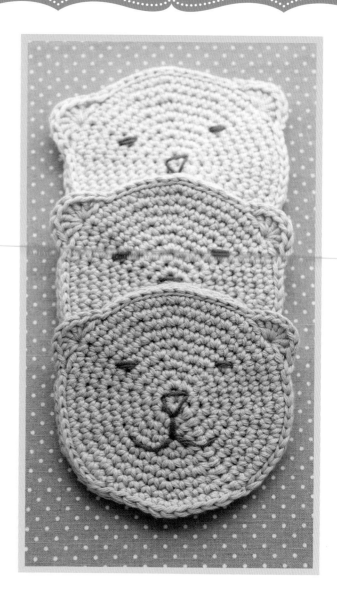 DMG Natura
Just Cotton (100% cotton; 1.75 ounces/
50 g = 170 yards/155 m): (B), 1 ball, color
tropic brown #22—approx 170 yards/
155 m of sock weight yarn
Note: You will not need a whole ball of
each color.

- Crochet hook: 4.5 mm (size 7 U.S.) or size
  to obtain gauge
- Yarn needle
- Embroidery needle

Gauge:
First 4 rnds = 10 inches/25.5 cm diameter
Always take time to check your gauge.

Stitches:
chain (ch)
slip stitch (sl st)
single crochet (sc)
double crochet (dc)

INSTRUCTIONS

CIRCLE (MAKE 2):

With A, make an adjustable ring.

Rnd 1: Work 6 sc in ring; join with sl st in first sc—6 sc.

Rnd 2: Ch 1, 2 sc in same st as joining, 2 sc in each st around; join with sl st in first sc—12 sc.

Rnd 3: Ch 1, sc in same st as joining, 2 sc in next st, *sc in next st, 2 sc in next st; rep from * around; join with sl st in first sc—18 sc.

Rnd 4: Ch 1, sc in same st as joining, 2 sc in next st, *sc in next 2 sts, 2 sc in next st; rep from * to last st, sc in last st; join with sl st in first sc—24 sc.

Rnd 5: Ch 1, sc in same st as joining, sc in next 2 sts, 2 sc in next st, *sc in next 3 sts, 2 sc in next st; rep from * around; join with sl st in first sc—30 sc.

Rnd 6: Ch 1, sc in same st as joining, sc in next st, 2 sc in next st, *sc in next 4 sts, 2 sc in next st; rep from * to last 2 sts, sc in last 2 sts; join with sl st in first sc—36 sc.

Rnd 7: Ch 1, sc in same st as joining, sc in next 4 sts, 2 sc in next st, *sc in next 5 sts, 2 sc in next st; rep from * around; join with sl st in first sc—42 sc.

Rnd 8: Ch 1, sc in same st as joining, sc in next 2 sts, 2 sts in next st, *sc in next 6 sts, 2 sts in next st; rep from * to last 3 sts, sc in last 3 sts; join with sl st in first sc—48 sc.

Rnd 9: Ch 1, sc in same st as joining, sc in next 6 sts, 2 sc in next st, *sc in next 7 sts, 2 sc in next st; rep from * around; join with sl st in first sc—54 sc.

Rnd 10: Ch 1, sc in same st as joining, sc in next 3 sts, 2 sts in next st, *sc in next 8 sts, 2 sts in next st; rep from * to last 4 sts, sc in next 4 sts; join with sl st in first sc—60 sc.

Fasten off and weave in ends.

JOIN CIRCLES AND MAKE EARS:

Place the two circles with WS together, matching stitches and aligning the seams where the rounds were joined.

Rnd 1: Working through both thicknesses, draw up a loop in first st following joining, sl st in next 12 sts, ch 1, sk next 2 sts, 6 dc in next st, ch 1 (first ear made), sk next 2 sts, sl st in next 15 sts, ch 1, sk next 2 sts, 6 dc in next st, ch 1 (2nd ear made), sk next 2 sts, sl st in next 13 sts; leave rem 10 sts unworked. Fasten off and weave in ends.

FINISHING:

Using photograph as a guide, with embroidery needle and B, embroider the face details on the front of the mitt, beginning with a triangle (for nose) in the center.

Darlin' Daisy Washcloths

Design by Jennifer Halvorson

Skill Level: Beginner
Finished Measurements:
8 inches/20.5 cm across at widest

Materials & Tools:
Lily Sugar 'n Cream (100% cotton;
2.5 ounces/70 g = 120 yards/109 m):
(A), 1 ball, color hot pink #01740;
(B), 1 ball, color hot blue #01742;
(C), 1 ball, color sunshine #00073;
(D), 1 ball, color blueberry #01725;
(E), 1 ball, color hot orange #01628—
approx 240 yards/218 m of worsted weight
yarn (for one cloth) 4 MEDIUM
Notes: Only two colors are needed
for each washcloth. You will not need
a whole ball of each color.

• Crochet hook: 6.00 mm (size J-10 U.S.)
  or size to obtain gauge
• Yarn Needle (optional)

Gauge:
Rnds 1–3 (center of daisy) measures
about 3½ inches/9 cm
Always take time to check your gauge.

Stitches:
chain (ch)
slip stitch (sl st)
single crochet (sc)
double crochet (dc)
half double crochet (hdc)
single crochet 3 together (sc3tog)

INSTRUCTIONS

With A, B, or E, ch 5; join with sl st in first ch to form a ring.

Rnd 1 (RS): Ch 2 (counts as first dc here and throughout), work 9 dc in ring; join with sl st in top of beg ch-2—10 dc.

Rnd 2: Ch 2, dc in same st as joining (first increase made), 2 dc in each st around; join with sl st in top of beg ch-2—20 dc.

Rnd 3: Ch 2, dc in same st as joining, dc in next st, *2 dc in next st, dc in next st; rep from * around; join with sl st in top of beg ch-2—30 dc. Fasten off.

Rnd 4: With RS facing, draw up a loop of A, C, or D in same st as joining, ch 2, dc in same st as joining, dc in next 2 sts, *2 dc in next st, dc in next 2 sts; rep from * around; join with sl st in top of beg ch-2—40 dc.

Rnd 5: Ch 2, dc in same st as joining, dc in next 4 sts, *2 dc in next st, dc in next 4 sts; rep from * around; join with sl st in top of beg ch-2—48 dc.

Rnd 6: Ch 1, *sk 1 st, 5 dc in next st (shell made), sk 1 st, sc in next st; rep from * around: join with sl st in beg ch-1—12 shells.

Rnd 7: Sl st in first dc, *hdc in next st, 3 hdc in next st, hdc in next st, sc3tog; rep from * around; join with sl st in first hdc.
Fasten off.

FINISHING:

Using a hook or yarn needle, weave in ends.
If desired, block washcloth to ensure that petals lie flat.

Owl Hooded Towel

Design by Kara Gunza

Skill Level: Easy
Finished Measurements:
Approx 26½ inches/67.5 cm square

Materials & Tools:
Bernat Handicrafter Cotton, Jumbo Size (100% cotton; 14 ounces/400 g = 710 yards/650 m): (A), 2 balls, color white #01—approx 1420 yards/1300 m of worsted weight yarn (4) MEDIUM
Lily Sugar 'n Cream (100% cotton; 2.5 ounces/ 71 g = 120 yards/109 m): (B), 1 ball, color black #00002; (C), 1 ball, soft violet #00093 OR aloe vera #25222; (D), 1 ball, rose pink #00046 OR hot blue #01742; (E), 1 ball, sunshine #00073—approx 480 yards/436 m of worsted weight yarn (4) MEDIUM
Note: You will not need a whole ball each of B, C, D, and E.

- Crochet hook: 5 mm (size H-8 U.S.) or size to obtain gauge
- Tapestry needle
- Stitch markers or safety pins (optional)

Gauge:
13 sts and 14 rows = 4 inches/10 cm, with A
Always take time to check your gauge.

Stitches:
chain (ch)
single crochet (sc)
single crochet 2 together (sc2tog)
single crochet 3 together (sc3tog)
slip stitch (sl st)
double crochet (dc)
treble crochet (tr)
long single crochet (Lsc)*

*SPECIAL STITCH NOTE
Long single crochet (Lsc): Insert hook in stitch of previous row. Draw up a loop to height of row being worked, complete as single crochet (the Lsc takes the place of the next stitch in the current row).

Notes:

1. Towel and hood are worked separately and then crocheted together.
2. Towel is worked from one corner diagonally across to the other corner. Stitches are increased to center diagonal (widest point), then decreased back down to opposite corner.
3. Eyes and beak are worked separately and sewn to hood. Eyes can be worked as flowery eyes or hoot-hoot eyes, as desired.

INSTRUCTIONS

TOWEL:

Tip: Here is a tip to make sure you are on the right track. The loops pulled up for each sc3tog should follow this sequence from the row below: sc, ch-sp, sc, except in Row 62, where the sequence from the row below would be ch-sp, sc, ch-sp.

With A, ch 2.

Foundation row: Work 3 sc in 2nd ch from hook—3 sc.

Row 1: Ch 1, turn, sc in first sc, beginning in same st as sc just made, sc2tog, ch 1, beginning in st where last loop was pulled up, sc2tog, sc in same st as last loop pulled up—5 sts.

Row 2: Ch 1, turn, sc in first st, beginning in same st as sc just made, sc2tog, ch 1, beginning in st where last loop was pulled up, sc3tog, ch 1, beginning in st where last loop was pulled up, sc2tog, sc in same st as last loop pulled up—7 sts.

Row 3: Ch 1, turn, sc in first sc, beginning in same st as sc just made, sc2tog, ch 1, *beginning in st where last loop was pulled up, sc3tog, ch 1; rep from * to last st, beginning in st where last loop was pulled up, sc2tog, sc in same st as last loop pulled up—9 sts.

Rows 4–61: Rep row 3 (each row will increase by 2 sts)—125 sts at the end of row 61.

Row 62: Ch 1, turn, sc3tog, *ch 1, beginning in st where last loop was pulled, sc3tog; rep from * across—123 sts.

Rows 63–121: Repeat row 62 (each row will decrease by 2 sts)—5 sts at the end of row 121.

Row 122: Ch 1, turn, sc3tog, ch 1, beginning in st where last loop was pulled, sc3tog—3 sts.

Fasten off and weave in ends.

HOOD:

Work same as towel through row 24—51 sts. Fasten off and weave in ends.

EYES (MAKE 2):

Option 1: Flowery Eyes:

With B, ch 2.

Foundation rnd (RS): Work 6 sc in 2nd ch from hook; join with sl st in first sc—6 sc. Fasten off.

Rnd 1: With RS facing, join C with sc in same st as joining, sc again in same st, 2 sc in each rem st around; join with sl st in first sc—12 sc. Fasten off.

Rnd 2: With RS facing, join D with sl st in same st as joining, ch 2, sk next st, *sl st in next st, ch 2, sk next st; rep from * around; join with sl st in first sl st—6 ch-2 sps.

Rnd 3: [Ch 1, (dc, 2 tr, dc) in next ch-2 sp (petal made), ch 1, sl st in next sl st] 6 times—6 petals. Fasten off, leaving a long tail for sewing eyes to hood.

Option 2: Hoot-Hoot Eyes:

With B, ch 2.

Foundation rnd (RS): Work 6 sc in 2nd ch from hook; join with sl st in first sc—6 sc. Fasten off.

Rnd 1 (RS): With RS facing, join C with sc in same st as joining, sc again in same st, 2 sc in each rem st around; join with sl st in first sc—12 sc. Fasten off.

Rnd 2: Ch 1, 2 sc in same st as joining, sc in next st, *2 sc in next st, sc in next st; rep from * around; join with sl st in first sc—18 sc. Fasten off.

Rnd 3: With RS facing, join D with sc in same st as joining, Lsc in next st 1 row below, *sc in next st, Lsc in next st 1 row below; rep from * around; join with sl st in first sc—18 sts. Fasten off.

Rnd 4: Ch 1, 2 sc in same st as joining, 2 sc in next st, sc in next st, *2 sc in each of next 2 sts, sc in next st; rep from * around, join with sl st in first sc—30 sc.

Fasten off, leaving a long tail for sewing eyes to hood.

BEAK:

With E, ch 2.

Foundation row: Work 2 sc in 2nd ch from hook—2 sts.

Row 1: Ch 1, turn, 2 sc in each st across—4 sts.

Row 2: Ch 1, turn, sc in each st across.

Row 3: Ch 1, turn, 2 sc in first st, sc in next 2 sts, 2 sc in last st—6 sts.

Row 4: Ch 1, turn, sc in each st across.

Edging:

Do not turn, beginning in same st as last sc made, sl st in end of each row down to tip of beak, (sl st, ch 1, sl st) in tip, sl st in end of each row back up, ending with sl st in the same st as first sc of row 4 was made; join with sl st in first sc of row 4.

Fasten off, leaving a long tail to sew beak to hood.

FINISHING:

Using photograph as a guide, with tapestry needle, sew eyes and beak to hood.

Edging:

Place hood on desired corner of towel, making sure rows match up (safety pin in place, if desired).

Joining Row: With RS facing, working through both thicknesses (hood and towel), join A with sc in edge at beginning of hood, sc in end of each row to top corner of hood, 3 sc in corner, sc in end of each row down side edge to end of hood; working through single thickness (towel only), *sc in end of each row to next corner, 3 sc in corner; rep from * 2 more times, sc in end of each row around; join with sl st in first sc.

Fasten off and weave in ends.

Ears:

Cut 2 pieces each of C, D, and E, each about 4 inches/10 cm long (you should have 6 lengths of yarn). With tapestry needle, pull each strand halfway through the stitch in desired location. Cut another length of yarn approximately the same length, gather strands pulled through stitch and use the last piece cut to tie around them. Trim to desired length.

Weave in any remaining ends.

Diaper Cover

Design by Shannon Graupman

Skill Level: Easy

Sizes:

0–3 months (3–6 months, 6–9 months, 9–12 months)

Finished Measurements:

Waist 16 (18, 20, 22) inches/41 (45.5, 51, 56) cm, buttoned at widest point

Length 10 (11 1/2, 13, 15) inches/25.5 (29, 33, 38) cm, measuring piece flat

Materials & Tools:

Caron Simply Soft (100% acrylic; 6 ounces/170 g = 315 yards/288 m): (A), 1 skein, color plum perfect #9761; (B), 1 skein, color grape #9610—approx 630 yards/576 m of worsted weight yarn

Note: You will not need a whole skein of each color.

- Crochet hook: 4.00 mm (size G-6 U.S.) or size to obtain gauge
- Yarn needle

Gauge:

16 hdc and 12 rows = 4 inches/10 cm
Always take time to check your gauge.

Stitches:

chain (ch)
half double crochet (hdc)
double crochet (dc)
half double crochet 2 together (hdc2tog)
single crochet (sc)
slip stitch (sl st)

Note:

Waist is adjustable. Button cover closes as snuggly as desired.

INSTRUCTIONS

With A, ch 48 (52, 56, 60).

Row 1: Hdc in 3rd ch from hook (beg ch does not count as a st) and each ch across—46 (50, 54, 58) sts.

Row 2: Ch 2 (does not count as a st here and throughout), turn, hdc in each st across.

Row 3 (buttonhole row): Ch 2, turn, dc in each st across.

Note: The spaces between the dc stitches of the previous row are to be used for buttonholes.

Rows 4 and 5: Ch 2, turn, hdc in each st across.

SHAPE LEG OPENINGS:

Row 6: Ch 1, turn, sl st in first 10 sts, ch 2, hdc in next 26 (30, 34, 38) sts; leave the rem 10 sts unworked—26 (30, 34, 38) hdc.

Row 7: Ch 2, turn, hdc in each st across.

Row 8: Ch 2, turn, hdc2tog, hdc in each st across to last 2 sts, hdc2tog—24 (28, 32, 36) hdc.

Rows 9–16: Rep last 2 rows 4 more times—16 (20, 24, 28) hdc at the end of row 16.

Rows 17–21 (26, 31, 36): Ch 2, turn, hdc in each st across.

Row 22 (27, 32, 37): Ch 2, turn, 2 hdc in first st, hdc in each st across to last st, 2 hdc in last st—18 (22, 26, 30) hdc.

Rows 23 (28, 33, 38)–26 (31, 36, 41): Rep last row 4 more times—26 (30, 34, 38) hdc.

Rows 27 (32, 37, 42)–30 (35, 40, 45): Ch 2, turn, hdc in each st across.

Fasten off.

EDGING:

With WS facing, join B with sl st anywhere in outer edge of cover, ch 1, sc in same sp as joining, sc evenly spaced all the way around the outside edge of cover; join with sl st in first sc. Fasten off.

CROCHET BUTTONS (MAKE 2):

With B, ch 2.

Rnd 1: 6 sc in 2nd ch from hook, taking care to work over the beginning tail; join with sl st in first sc. Pull on the beginning tail to close the center opening.

Rnd 2: Ch 1, 2 sc in each sc around; join with sl st in first sc—12 sc.

Fasten off.

FINISHING:

With B, sew buttons to front of cover. Use spaces between double crochet stitches for buttonholes. Weave in ends.

Soaker

Design by Shannon Gilbride

BATH TIME

Skill Level: Easy

Sizes:

Newborn (Small, Medium, Large)

Finished Measurements:

Hip Circumference 17 (19, 21, 23)
inches/43 (48.5, 53.5, 58.5) cm

Materials and Tools:

Red Heart Soft (100% acrylic; 5
ounces/141 g = 256 yards/234 m): 1 ball,
color teal #9518—approx 256 yards/
234 m of worsted weight yarn [4 MEDIUM]

- Crochet hooks: 4.5 mm (size 7 U.S.) and 5
  mm (size H-8 U.S.) or size to obtain gauge
- Yarn needle
- Stitch markers

Gauge:

16 sts and 16 rows = 4 inches/10 cm over
single crochet using larger hook
Always take time to check your gauge.

Stitches:

single crochet (sc)
chain (ch)
slip stitch (sl st)
half double crochet (hdc)
half double crochet 2 together (hdc2tog)
back post half double crochet (BPhdc)*
front post half double crochet (FPhdc)*

Notes:

1. Work this pattern by crocheting the waistband in a ribbed pattern, crocheting the hip area, then the gusset, and finishing with ribbed leg openings.
2. To accommodate diapers and bellies, you will work in some short rows, which provide extra room in the back. Short rows are rows in which stitches are only worked over a portion of the stitches in the previous row or round; the remaining stitches are left unworked temporarily. Later, stitches are worked over all stitches (including those that were left unworked previously).
3. A drawstring will finish off your soaker.
4. The ch-1 at the beginning of each round and row does not count as a stitch. Take care not to work into this chain when working the next round or row.
5. One ball of the indicated yarn is sufficient to make a soaker in any of the sizes listed.

*SPECIAL STITCHES

Back Post half double crochet (BPhdc):
Yarn over, insert hook from back to front to back again around post of indicated stitch, yarn over and draw up a loop, yarn over and draw through all 3 loops on hook.

Front Post half double crochet (FPhdc):
Yarn over, insert hook from front to back to front again around post of indicated stitch, yarn over and draw up a loop, yarn over and draw through all 3 loops on hook.

41

INSTRUCTIONS

WAIST BAND:

With smaller hook, ch 9.

Row 1: Working in back loops only, sc in 2nd ch from hook and in each ch across—8 sc.

Rows 2–60 (68, 76, 86): Ch 1, turn, sc in each sc across.

Do not fasten off.

Fold the waistband, bringing first row up and behind last row made.

Joining row: Ch 1, working through both thicknesses (through sts of last row and into chains across opposite side of the foundation ch at the same time), sl st in each st across to join waistband into a circle.

Do not fasten off.

HIPS:

Turn the waistband so that the seam is on the inside. Work the next round across one long edge of the waistband circle. Work now proceeds in rounds for a few rounds.

Rnd 1 (RS): Ch 1 (does not count as a st here and throughout), turn, working in ends of rows around one long edge of waistband circle, *hdc in next 6 (7, 8, 12) sts, 2 hdc in next st; rep from * to last 4 (4, 4, 8) sts, hdc in last 4 (4, 4, 8) sts; join with sl st in first hdc—68 (76, 84, 92) hdc.

Note: If you wish to change colors at this point, you may finish off the waist color and start a new color in the first stitch.

Change to larger hook.

Rnd 2: Ch 1, turn, hdc in first 34 (38, 42, 46) sts, place marker to indicate right hip, hdc in last 34 (38, 42, 46) sts; join with sl st in first hdc.

Move marker up as each round is worked.

SHAPE BACKSIDE WITH SHORT ROWS:

Work now proceeds back and forth in rows worked over only a portion of the stitches in the previous round or row (short rows).

Short row 1 (RS): Ch 1, turn, hdc in first 31 (35, 39, 43) sts; leave remaining sts unworked.

Short row 2 (WS): Ch 1, turn, hdc2tog, hdc in next 26 (30, 34, 38) sts; leave last 3 sts of previous row unworked.

You will now work into all of the stitches (including the unworked stitches) to return to the beginning of short row 1 and resume working in rounds.

Rnd 3 (RS): Ch 1, turn, hdc2tog, hdc in each st to end of short row, hdc in the SIDE of the short rows, hdc in each unworked st to beginning of short row 1; join with sl st in first hdc.

Rnd 4 (WS): Ch 1, turn, hdc in next st around to end of short row, hdc in the SIDE of the short rows, hdc in the 3 remaining unworked sts of the short rows; join with sl st in first hdc—68 (76, 84, 92) sts.

Note: What you have done here is add two rows to the back of the soaker, while only adding one row to the front. While working the short rows, hdc2tog decreases are worked twice and then stitches are worked into the sides of the short rows, closing up any gap, and ensuring that the same number of stitches are still worked all the way around.

Rnds 5 and 6: Ch 1, turn, hdc in each st around; join with sl st in first hdc.

Rep short row 1, short row 2, and rnds 3–6 until back of soaker is about 1 (2, 2, 3) inches/2.5 (5, 5, 7.5) cm longer than the front. This will allow for good coverage over the backside and room for your little one's tummy in the front.

Next rnd: Ch 1, turn, hdc in each hdc around; join with sl st in first hdc.

Rep last rnd until soaker measures about 13 (13, 14, 14) inches/33 (33, 35.5, 35.5) cm in rise (the measurement achieved by measuring down the front and back up the backside). For example, when the front is 6 inches/15 cm and the back is 8 inches/20.5 cm, the rise is 14 inches/35.5 cm. End on a WS row, no-short-row, round. Fasten off.

GUSSET:

Lay the soaker down in front of you right side up with the marker on your left. Now you are going to measure out the thighs and crochet the crotch gusset to make the leg openings.

Counting left to right from the marker, count 10 (12, 14, 16) sts, and place a marker (1st gusset marker). Count 14 sts, and place another marker (2nd gusset marker). To place the markers on the back, flip the soaker over so the back is facing you, and count out and mark the back in the same manner as the front. Now you may remove the hip marker. You should have 14 sts between each set of markers.

Row 1 (RS): With RS of front facing, join yarn with sl st 1 st to the left of the first gusset marker, ch 1, hdc in the same st, hdc in next 13 sts to next gusset marker—14 sts.

Row 2: Ch 1, turn, hdc in each st across.

Rep last row until gusset measures about 2 (3, 3, 4) inches/5 (7.5, 7.5, 10) cm; end with a RS row. Turn the soaker inside out, match the sts on the last row of the gusset with the sts between the gusset markers on the back. Ch 1, working through both thicknesses, sl st in each st across to join front and back together. Fasten off, remove all markers, and turn the soaker right side out.

RIBBED CUFFS:

Lay soaker out so that the gusset is folded perfectly in half, and find the middle of the gusset.

First leg:

Rnd 1 (RS): With RS facing, join yarn with sl st in the edge at the middle of the gusset, ch 1, work hdc evenly spaced around edge of leg opening and making sure that you work an even number of hdc sts; join with sl st in first hdc.

Note: To get an even number of hdc stitches worked around the leg edge, I usually work one hdc in the side of each gusset row, then one hdc in each stitch around. Working about 30 (34, 38, 42) sts.

Rnds 2–3 (5, 5, 5): Ch 1, turn, *FPhdc around next st, BPhdc around next st; rep from 8* around; join with sl st in first st.

Fasten off.

Second leg:

Work ribbed cuff around second leg opening in same manner as ribbed cuff for first leg.

FINISHING:

Weave in ends.

Drawstring:

With 2 strands of yarn held together, work chains until piece measures about 30 (32, 34, 36) inches/76 (81, 86.5, 91.5) cm long, or desired length. Fasten off. Weave drawstring through the small openings around the waistband where the ribbing meets the main body, with the ends meeting in the front, and knot the ends, trimming to desired length. Tie ends of drawstring into a bow.

Bear Hat

Design by Julie Barber

Skill Level: Easy

Sizes:

0–3 months (3–6 months, 6–9 months, 9–12 months)

Finished Measurements:

Circumference 11½ (13, 15, 16) inches/ 29 (33, 38, 40.5) cm, unstretched

Materials & Tools:

Hobby Lobby Andes Alpaca (85% acrylic, 15% alpaca; 3.5 ounces/100 g = 120 yards/ 109 m): (A), 1 ball, color truffle #722; (B), 1 ball, color peacock #710—approx 240 yards/218 m of worsted weight yarn 🧶**4 MEDIUM**

- Crochet hooks: 3.75 mm (size F-5 U.S.) (for ears only) and 5.5 mm (size I-9 U.S.) or size to obtain gauge
- Yarn Needle

Gauge:

15 hdc and 8 rnds = 4 inches/10 cm with larger hook

Always take time to check your gauge.

Stitches:

chain (ch)
double crochet (dc)
slip stitch (sl st)
Front Post double crochet (FPdc)*
Back Post double crochet (BPdc)*
single crochet (sc)
half double crochet (dc)
crossed-dc*

Notes:

Hat is worked in joined rounds, beginning at the top of the hat.

Hat will stretch slightly to fit a range of sizes.

INSTRUCTIONS

SIZE 0–3 MONTHS ONLY:

With larger hook and A, ch 3.

Rnd 1 (RS): Work 11 dc in 3rd ch from hook (beg ch does not count as a st); join with sl st in first dc—11 dc.

Rnd 2: Ch 2 (does not count as a st here and throughout), 2 dc in each st around; join with sl st in first dc—22 dc.

*SPECIAL STITCHES

Front Post double crochet (FPdc): Yarn over, insert hook from front to back to front again around post of indicated stitch, yarn over and draw up a loop, [yarn over and draw through 2 loops on hook] twice.

Back Post double crochet (BPdc): Yarn over, insert hook from back to front to back again around post of indicated stitch, yarn over and draw up a loop, [yarn over and draw through 2 loops on hook] twice.

Crossed-dc: Skip next st, dc in next st, dc in skipped st.

Rnd 3: Ch 2, [2 dc in next dc, dc in next dc] 11 times; join with sl st in first dc—33 dc.

Rnd 4: Ch 2, [2 dc in next dc, dc in next 2 dc] 11 times; join with sl st in first dc—44 dc.

Rnds 5–7: Ch 3 (counts as first dc here and throughout), dc in last st of previous rnd (first crossed-dc made), [crossed-dc] 21 times; join with sl st in sp between beg ch-3 and first dc—22 crossed-dc.

Rnd 8: Ch 2, sk first dc, dc in each rem dc around; join with sl st in top of beg ch-2—43 dc. Fasten off A.

Rnd 9: With RS facing, draw up a loop of B in joining sl st, ch 2, FPdc around first dc, *BPdc around next dc, FPdc around next dc; rep from * around; join with sl st in top of beg ch-2.

Rnd 10: Ch 2, FPdc around first FPdc, *BPdc around next BPdc, FPdc around next FPdc; rep from * around; join with sl st in top of beg ch-2. Fasten off.

SIZE 3–6 MONTHS ONLY:

With larger hook and A, ch 2.

Rnd 1 (RS): Work 6 sc in 2nd ch from hook; join with sl st in first sc—6 sc.

Rnd 2: Ch 2 (does not count as a st here and throughout), 2 dc in each st around; join with sl st in first dc—12 dc.

Rnd 3: Ch 2, 2 dc in each st around; join with sl st in first dc—24 dc.

Rnd 4: Ch 2, [2 dc in next dc, dc in next dc] 12 times; join with sl st in first dc—36 dc.

Rnd 5: Ch 2, [2 dc in next dc, dc in next 2 dc] 12 times; join with sl st in first dc—48 dc.

Rnds 6–9: Ch 3 (counts as first dc here and throughout), dc in last st of previous rnd (first

crossed-dc made), [crossed-dc] 23 times; join with sl st in sp between beg ch-3 and first dc—24 crossed-dc.

Rnd 10: Ch 2, sk first dc, dc in each rem dc around; join with sl st in top of beg ch-2—47 dc. Fasten off A.

Rnd 11: With RS facing, draw up a loop of B in joining sl st, ch 2, FPdc around first dc, *BPdc around next dc, FPdc around next dc; rep from * around; join with sl st in top of beg ch-2.

Rnd 12: Ch 2, FPdc around first FPdc, *BPdc around next BPdc, FPdc around next FPdc; rep from * around; join with sl st in top of beg ch-2. Fasten off.

SIZE 6–9 MONTHS ONLY:

With larger hook and A, ch 2.

Rnd 1 (RS): Work 7 sc in 2nd ch from hook; join with sl st in first sc—7 sc.

Rnd 2: Ch 2 (does not count as a st here and throughout), 2 dc in each st around; join with sl st in first dc—14 dc.

Rnd 3: Ch 2, 2 dc in each st around; join with sl st in first dc—28 dc.

Rnd 4: Ch 2, [2 dc in next dc, dc in next dc] 14 times; join with sl st in first dc—42 dc.

Rnd 5: Ch 2, [2 dc in next dc, dc in next 2 dc] 14 times; join with sl st in first dc—56 dc.

Rnds 6–9: Ch 3 (counts as first dc here and throughout), dc in last st of previous rnd (first crossed-dc made), [crossed-dc] 27 times; join with sl st in sp between beg ch-3 and first dc—28 crossed-dc.

Rnd 10: Ch 2, sk first dc, dc in each rem dc around; join with sl st in top of beg ch-2—55 dc. Fasten off A.

Rnd 11: With RS facing, draw up a loop of B in joining sl st, ch 2, FPdc around first dc, *BPdc around next dc, FPdc around next dc; rep from * around; join with sl st in top of beg ch-2.

Rnds 12–14: Ch 2, FPdc around first FPdc, *BPdc around next BPdc, FPdc around next FPdc; rep from * around; join with sl st in top of beg ch-2. Fasten off.

SIZE 9–12 MONTHS ONLY:

With larger hook and A, ch 2.

Rnd 1 (RS): Work 8 sc in 2nd ch from hook; join with sl st in first sc—8 sc.

Rnd 2: Ch 2 (does not count as a st here and throughout), dc in first dc, 2 dc in each rem dc around; join with sl st in first dc—15 dc.

Rnd 3: Ch 2, 2 dc in each st around; join with sl st in first dc—30 dc.

Rnd 4: Ch 2, [2 dc in next dc, dc in next dc] 15 times; join with sl st in first dc—45 dc.

Rnd 5: Ch 2, [2 dc in next dc, dc in next 2 dc] 15 times; join with sl st in first dc—60 dc.

Rnds 6–9: Ch 3 (counts as first dc here and throughout), dc in last st of previous rnd (first crossed-dc made), [crossed-dc] 29 times; join with sl st in sp between beg ch-3 and first dc—30 crossed-dc.

Rnd 10: Ch 2, sk first dc, dc in each rem dc around; join with sl st in top of beg ch-2—55 dc. Fasten off A.

Rnd 11: With RS facing, draw up a loop of B in joining sl st, ch 2, FPdc around first dc, *BPdc around next dc, FPdc around next dc; rep from * around; join with sl st in top of beg ch-2.

Rnds 12–14: Ch 2, FPdc around first FPdc, *BPdc around next BPdc, FPdc around next FPdc; rep from * around; join with sl st in top of beg ch-2. Fasten off.

ALL SIZES:

Bear Ears (make 2):
Inner Ear (make 1 for each ear):
With smaller hook and B, ch 2.

Rnd 1: Work 8 hdc in 2nd ch from hook; do not join, work in continuous rnds—8 hdc.

Rnd 2: Work 2 hdc in next 8 hdc; join with sl st in next st—16 hdc.
Fasten off.

Outer Ear (make 1 for each ear):
With smaller hook and B, ch 2.

Rnd 1: Work 8 hdc in 2nd ch from hook; do not join, work in continuous rnds—8 hdc.

Rnd 2: Work 2 hdc in next 8 hdc—16 hdc.

Rnd 3: Place one inner ear on top of this outer ear, matching sts; working through both thicknesses, [2 hdc in next st, hdc into next st] 8 times—24 hdc.

Rnd 4: Hdc in next 18 hdc; leave rem sts unworked (for lower edge of ear).
Fasten off, leaving a long tail for sewing.

FINISHING:

Use the long yarn tails to sew ears to each side of top of hat. Weave in any remaining ends.

Monster Hat

Design by Heather Main

Size Toddler ONLY:

Rnd 7: Ch 1, [hdc in next 5 sts, 2 hdc in next st] 8 times; join with sl st in first hdc—56 hdc.

Rnd 8: Ch 1, [hdc in next 13 sts, 2 hdc in next st] 4 times; join with sl st in first hdc—60 hdc.

ALL Sizes:

Rnds 7 (8, 8, 9)–16 (18, 18, 20): Ch 1, hdc in each st around; join with sl st in first hdc—48 (52, 56, 60) hdc.

Do not fasten off.

FIRST EARFLAP:

Row 1: Ch 1, turn, sc in next 8 (8, 10, 10) sc; leave rem sts unworked—8 (8, 10, 10) sc.

Row 2: Ch 1, turn, sk first sc, sc in next 7 (7, 9, 9) sc—7 (7, 9, 9) sc.

Rows 3–7 (7, 9, 9): Ch 1, turn, sk first sc, sc in each rem sc of previous row—2 sc at the end of row 7 (7, 9, 9).

Row 8 (8, 10, 10): Ch 1, turn, sk first sc, sc in last sc—1 sc.

Fasten off.

SECOND EARFLAP:

With RS facing, sk 18 unworked sts of last rnd of hat following first earflap, draw up a loop of A in next st.

Row 1: Ch 1, sc in next 8 (8, 10, 10) sc; leave rem sts unworked—8 (8, 10, 10) sc.

Rows 2–8 (8, 10, 10): Work same as rows 2–8 (8, 10, 10) of first earflap.

Fasten off.

EDGING:

Note: The back lower edge of the hat is the shortest lower edge between the two earflaps. The longer section between earflaps is the front of the hat.

With RS facing, join D with sc in any st of back lower edge of hat, sc evenly spaced all the way around lower edge, working 3 sc in point of each earflap; join with sl st in first sc. Fasten off.

SMALL HORNS (MAKE 3):

With C, make an adjustable ring.

Rnd 1: Ch 1, 4 sc in ring; join with sl st in first sc—4 sc.

Rnd 2: Ch 1, [sc in next st, 2 sc in next st] twice; join with sl st in first sc—6 sc.

Rnd 3: Ch 1, [sc in next 2 sts, 2 sc in next st] twice; join with sl st in first sc—8 sc.

Rnd 4: Ch 1, [sc in next 3 sts, 2 sc in next st] twice; join with sl st in first sc—10 sc.

Rnd 5: Ch 1, [sc in next 4 sts, 2 sc in next st] twice; join with sl st in first sc—12 sc.

Rnds 6 and 7: Ch 1, sc in each st around; join with sl st in first sc.

Fasten off, leaving a long tail for sewing horn to top of hat.

TALL HORNS (MAKE 2):

With B, make an adjustable ring.

Rnds 1–4: Work same as rnds 1–4 of small horns—10 sc at the end of rnd 4.

Rnds 5–11: Ch 1, sc in each st around; join with sl st in first sc.

Fasten off, leaving a long tail for sewing horn to top of hat.

LARGE EYE:

With C, make an adjustable ring.

Rnd 1 (RS): Ch 1, 8 hdc in ring; join with sl st in first hdc—8 hdc.

Rnd 2: Ch 1, 2 hdc in each st around; join with sl st in first hdc—16 hdc. Fasten off C.

Rnd 3: With RS facing, draw up a loop of B in same st as joining sl st, ch 1, *[hdc in next st, 2 hdc in next st] twice, [dc in next st, 2 dc in next st] twice; rep from * once more; join with sl st in first hdc—24 sts.

Rnd 4: Ch 1, *[hdc in next 2 sts, 2 hdc in next st] twice, [dc in next 2 sts, 2 dc in next st] twice; rep from * once more; join with sl st in first hdc—32 sts. Fasten off, leaving a long tail for sewing eye to hat.

SMALL EYE:

With D, make an adjustable ring.

Rnd 1 (RS): Ch 1, 6 hdc in ring; join with sl st in first hdc—6 hdc.

Rnd 2: Ch 1, 2 hdc in each st around; join with sl st in first hdc—12 hdc.

Rnd 3: Ch 1, [hdc in next st, 2 hdc in next st] 6 times; join with sl st in first hdc—18 hdc. Fasten off, leaving a long tail for sewing eye to hat. Embroider eye with an X using one strand of yarn doubled over.

FINISHING:

Sew button onto center of the large eye. With a doubled strand of C, embroider an X near the center of the small eye. Sew eyes to front of hat. With C and using photograph as a guide, embroider a straight stitch zigzag below eyes for mouth. Stuff horns lightly with fiberfill. Sew small horn centered on the top of the hat, then a tall horn on each side of the small horn, using the ear flaps to center the horns' positioning. Sew two remaining short horns on each side of the tall horns.

Braids:

Cut 6 lengths of A, B, C, and D, each 60 inches/ 152.5 cm long. Hold 3 lengths of each color together and fold in half. Insert crochet hook in tip of one earflap, place fold on hook, and draw through to form a loop. Thread the ends through the loop, draw the ends all the way through, and pull to tighten. Divide the strands into 3 equal groups and braid the groups together. Tie an overhand knot at the end of the braid to secure, leaving about 1½ inches/4 cm unbraided for tassel. Rep with remaining 3 lengths to attach braid to other earflap.

Weave in any remaining ends.

Pixie Gnome Hat

Design by Lori Jo Shoemake

Skill Level: Easy

Sizes:

0–3 months (3–6 months, 6–12 months, 12 months–2 years)

Finished Measurements:

Circumference 12 (13, 16, 18) inches/30.5 (33, 40.5, 45.5) cm, unstretched

Materials & Tools:

For Striped Hat:

Lily Sugar 'n Cream (100% cotton; 2.5 ounces/71 g = 120 yards/109 m): (A), 1 ball, color hot green #01712; (B), 1 ball, color dark pine #00016; (D), 1 ball, color white #00001; (E), 1 ball, color yellow #0010; (F), 1 ball, color red #0095—approx 600 yards/545 m of worsted weight yarn 4 MEDIUM

Peaches & Crème (100% cotton; 2.5 ounces/70.9 g = 120 yards/109 m): (C), 1 ball, color bright blue #01742; (G), 1 ball, color bright orange #01628—approx 240 yards/218 m of worsted weight yarn 4 MEDIUM

Note: You will not need a whole ball of each color.

For Solid-Color Hat:

Lion Brand Lion Cotton (100% cotton; 5 ounces/140 g = 236 yards/212 m): (H), 1 ball, color natural #98—approx 236 yards/212 m of worsted weight yarn 4 MEDIUM

Lily Sugar 'n Cream (100% cotton; 2.5 ounces/71 g = 120 yards/109 m): (D), 1 ball, color white #00001—approx 120 yards/109 m of worsted weight yarn 4 MEDIUM

For Flower Embellishment (see page 54):

Lily Sugar 'n Cream (100% cotton; 2.5 ounces/71 g = 120 yards/109 m): (D), 1 ball, color white #00001; (I), small amount, color #00046 rose pink—approx 120 yards/109 m of worsted weight yarn 4 MEDIUM

Note: You will not need a whole ball of each color.

- **Crochet hooks:**
  Size 0–3 months: 3.75 mm (size F-5 U.S.)
  Size 3–6 months: 4 mm (size G-6 U.S)
  Size 6–12 months and Flower Embellishment: 5 mm (size H-8 U.S.)
  Size 12 months–2 years: 5.5 mm (size I-9 U.S.)
- **Yarn needle**

Gauge:

16 sts = 4 inches/10cm with 3.75 mm (size F-5 U.S.) hook
14 sts = 3¾ inches/9.5cm with 4 mm (size G-6 U.S.) hook
12 sts = 4 inches/10cm with 5 mm (size H-8 U.S.) hook
10 sts = 3¾ inches/9.5 cm with 5.5 (size I-9 U.S.) hook
Always take time to check your gauge.

Stitches:

chain (ch)
slip stitch (sl st)
double crochet (dc)
single crochet (sc)

hook, ch 2 more with new color to create first dc for this new round, continue with pattern as instructed.

INSTRUCTIONS

HAT:

With appropriate size hook for desired size and A, ch 4; join with a sl st in first ch to form a ring.

Rnd 1: Ch 2 (counts as first dc here and throughout), work 5 more dc in ring; join with sl st in top of beg ch-2—6 dc (this forms the point at the top of the hat).

Rnd 2: Ch 2, 2 dc in next st, [dc in next st, 2 dc in next st] twice; join with sl st in top of beg ch-2—9 dc. Change to B.

Rnd 3: With B, ch 2, dc in next st, 2 dc in next st, [dc in next 2 sts, 2 dc in next st] twice; join with sl st in top of beg ch-2—12 dc. Change to C.

Rnd 4: With C, ch 2, dc in next 2 sts, 2 dc in next st, [dc in next 3 sts, 2 dc in next st] twice; join with sl st in top of beg ch-2—15 dc. Change to D.

Rnd 5: With D, ch 2, dc in next 3 sts, 2 dc in next st, [dc in next 4 sts, 2 dc in next st] twice; join with sl st in top of beg ch-2—18 dc. Change to E.

Rnd 6: With E, ch 2, dc in next 4 sts, 2 dc in next st, [dc in next 5 sts, 2 dc in next st] twice; join with sl st in top of beg ch-2—21 dc. Change to F.

Rnd 7: With F, ch 2, dc in next 5 sts, 2 dc in next st, [dc in next 6 sts, 2 dc in next st] twice; join with sl st in top of beg ch-2—24 dc. Do not change color.

Rnd 8: With F, ch 2, 2 dc in next st, *dc in next st, 2 dc in next st; rep from * around; join with sl st in top of beg ch-2—36 dc. Change to G.

Rnd 9: With G, ch 2, dc in next st, 2 dc in next st,

Notes:

1. Hat can be worked in stripes, changing color every few rounds as in instructions, or in a single color. To make hat in a single color, do not change color, work all rounds and rows with H and work edging with D.

2. Hat is worked the same for all sizes. Different size hooks result in different size hats.

3. To obtain an almost invisible seam and transition when changing colors, try this technique: At end of round, insert hook into top chain of beg ch-3 but DO NOT pull through a loop. Cut yarn to approximately 4 inches/10 cm, and let hang. Attach next color to hook and pull loop through, tie new color to previous color tail snuggly and close to

*dc in next 2 sts, 2 dc in next st; rep from * around; join with sl st in top of beg ch-2—48 dc. Change to D.

Rnd 10: With D, ch 2, dc in each st around; join with sl st in top of beg ch-2. Change to B.

Rnd 11: With B, ch 2, dc in each st around; join with sl st in top of beg ch-2. Change to E.

Rnd 12: With E, ch 2, dc in each st around; join with sl st in top of beg ch-2. Do not change color.

Rnds 13 and 14: With E, ch 2, dc in each st around; join with sl st in top of beg ch-2. Change to F at the end of rnd 14.

Rnd 15: With F, ch 2, dc in each st around; join with sl st in top of beg ch-2.
Fasten off.

First Earflap:

Row 1 (RS): With RS facing, sk 5 sts following the joining seam, draw up a loop of C in next st, ch 3 (counts as first dc here and throughout earflaps), sk next st, dc in next 8 sts, sk next st, dc in next st; leave rem sts unworked—10 dc.

Rows 2–4: Ch 3, turn, sk next st, dc in each st across to 1 st before beg ch-3, sk next st, dc in top of beg ch-3—4 dc at end of row 4.

Row 5: Ch 3, turn, sk next 2 sts, dc in top of beg ch-3. Fasten off.

Second Ear Flap:

Row 1 (RS): With RS facing, sk 15 sts before the joining seam, draw up a loop of C in the st before the skipped sts, ch 3, sk next st, dc in next 8 sts, sk next st, dc in next st; leave rem sts unworked—10 dc.

Rows 2–5: Work same as rows 2–5 of first earflap. Fasten off.

EDGING:

Rnd 1 (RS): With RS facing, draw up a loop of D in joining seam, ch 1, *sc in each sc to earflap; work 2 sc in end of each row up side of earflap, 4 sc in tip of earflap, 2 sc in end of each row down other side of earflap; rep from * once more, sc in each rem sc around; join with sl st in first sc. Fasten off.

FLOWER EMBELLISHMENT (OPTIONAL):

With D, ch 4; join with sl st in first ch to form a ring.

Rnd 1: [Ch 3, sc in ring] 6 times—6 sc and 6 ch-3 sps.

Rnd 2: (Sc, ch 1, 3 dc, ch 1, sc) in each ch-3 sp around—6 petals.

Rnd 3: Push petals forward and work this round behind the petals, [sc around next sc of rnd 1, ch 4] 6 times; join with sl st in first sc—6 sc and 6 ch-4 sps.

Rnd 4: (sc, ch 1, 5 dc, ch 1, sc) in each ch-4 sp around—6 petals.

Fasten off, leaving a long tail for sewing or tying flower to hat. If flower is tied to hat, it can be removed whenever desired.

Tip: For additional rounds of petals, rep rnd 3, increasing the number of chains in each chain-space by 1, then rep rnd 4, increasing the number of dc stitches by 2.

Center:

Roll length of I into a small yarn ball, and sew ball to center of flower. A small button could also be used for center of flower.

FINISHING:

Sew or tie flower embellishment to hat. Weave in any remaining ends.

Pom-pom Hat

Design by Imge Tekuz

Skill Level: Beginner

Sizes:

0–3 months (3–6 months, 6–12 months, 12–24 months, 2T–4T)

Finished Measurements:

Circumference 13½ (14, 15, 16, 17, 18) inches/34.5 (35.5, 38, 40.5, 43, 45.5) cm

Materials & Tools:

Anchor Olimpos (100% acrylic; 3.53 ounces/100 g = 142 yards/130 m): (A), 1 ball, color aqua blue; (B), 1 ball, color light orange; (C), 1 ball, color fuschia; (D), 1 ball, color purple; (E), 1 ball, color light blue; (F), 1 ball, color bright orange—approx 142 yards/130 m bulky weight yarn [5 BULKY]

Note: You will not need a whole ball of each color.

- Crochet hook: 5 mm (size H-8 U.S.) or size to obtain gauge
- Yarn needle
- Pom-pom maker

Gauge:

11 hdc and 8 rows = 4 inches/10 cm. Always take time to check your gauge.

Stitches:

chain (ch)
half double crochet (hdc)
slip stitch (sl st)
reverse single crochet stitch (rsc)

Notes:

1. Hat is worked in joined rounds with right side always facing and beginning at the top of the hat.
2. Earflaps are worked back and forth in rows, beginning over a section of the last round of the hat.

INSTRUCTIONS

With A, make an adjustable ring.

Rnd 1 (RS): Ch 2 (counts as first hdc here and throughout), work 8 hdc in ring, pull tail gently but firmly to close ring; join with sl st in top of beg ch—9 hdc.

Rnd 2: Ch 2, hdc in same st as joining (increase made), 2 hdc in each st around; join with sl st in top of beg ch—18 hdc.

Rnd 3: Ch 2, hdc in same st as joining, hdc in next st, *2 hdc in next st, hdc in next st; rep from * around; join with sl st in top of beg ch—27 hdc.

Rnd 4: Ch 2, hdc in same st as joining, hdc in next 2 sts, *2 hdc in next st, hdc in next 2 sts; rep from * around; join with sl st in top of beg ch—36 hdc.

SIZE NEWBORN ONLY:

Rnd 5: Ch 2, hdc in each st around; join with sl st in top of beg ch. Fasten off A.

Rnd 6 (RS): With RS facing, join B with sl st in same st as joining, ch 2, hdc in each st around; join with sl st in top of beg ch. Fasten off B.

Rnd 7: With C, rep rnd 6. Fasten off C.

Rnd 8: With D, rep rnd 6. Fasten off D.

Rnd 9: With E, rep rnd 6. Fasten off E.

Right Earflap:

Row 1 (RS): With RS facing, sk 3 sts following back seam, join E with sl st in next st, ch 2, hdc in next 7 sts; leave rem sts unworked—8 hdc.

Row 2: Ch 2, turn, hdc in each st across.

Row 3: Ch 2, turn, sk next st, hdc in rem 6 hdc—7 hdc.

Row 4: Ch 2, turn, sk next st, hdc in rem 5 hdc—6 hdc.

Row 5: Ch 2, turn, sk next st, hdc in next 3 hdc, sk next st, sl st in last st. Fasten off.

Left Earflap:

Row 1 (RS): With RS facing, sk 14 sts following right earflap, join E with sl st in next st, ch 2, hdc in next 7 sts; leave rem sts unworked—8 hdc.

Rows 2–5: Work same as rows 2–5 of right earflap. Fasten off.

SIZE 0–3 MONTHS ONLY:

Rnd 5: Ch 2, hdc in same st as joining, hdc in next 8 sts, *2 hdc in next st, hdc in next 8 sts; rep from * around; join with sl st in top of beg ch—40 hdc.

Rnd 6 (RS): With RS facing, join B with sl st in same st as joining, ch 2, hdc in each st around; join with sl st in top of beg ch. Fasten off B.

Rnd 7: With C, rep rnd 6. Fasten off C.

Rnd 8: With D, rep rnd 6.

Rnd 9: Continuing with D, ch 2, hdc in each st around; join with sl st in top of beg ch. Fasten off D.

Rnd 10: With E, rep rnd 6. Fasten off E.

Right Earflap:

Row 1 (RS): With RS facing, sk 3 sts following back seam, join E with sl st in next st, ch 2, hdc in next 7 sts; leave rem sts unworked—8 hdc.

Row 2: Ch 2, turn, sk first st, hdc in each st across.

Row 3: Ch 2, turn, sk first st, hdc in next 6 hdc—7 hdc.

Row 4: Ch 2, turn, sk first st, hdc in next 5 hdc—6 hdc.

Row 5: Ch 2, turn, sk first st, hdc in next 3 hdc, sk next st, sl st in last st. Fasten off.

Left Earflap:

Row 1 (RS): With RS facing, sk 18 sts following right earflap, join E with sl st in next st, ch 2, hdc in next 7 sts; leave rem sts unworked—8 hdc.

Rows 2–5: Work same as rows 2–5 of right earflap. Fasten off.

SIZE 3–6 MONTHS ONLY:

Rnd 5: Ch 2, hdc in same st as joining, hdc in next 5 sts, *2 hdc in next st, hdc in next 5 sts; rep from * around; join with sl st in top of beg ch—42 hdc.

Rnd 6 (RS): With RS facing, join B with sl st in same st as joining, ch 2, hdc in each st around; join with sl st in top of beg ch. Fasten off B.

Rnd 7: With C, rep rnd 6. Fasten off C.

Rnd 8: With D, rep rnd 6.

Rnd 9: Continuing with D, ch 2, hdc in each st around; join with sl st in top of beg ch. Fasten off D.

Rnd 10: With E, rep rnd 6. Fasten off E.

Right Earflap:

Row 1 (RS): With RS facing, sk 4 sts following back seam, join E with sl st in next st, ch 2, hdc in next 8 sts; leave rem sts unworked—9 hdc.

Row 2: Ch 2, turn, sk first st, hdc in each st across.

Row 3: Ch 2, turn, sk first st, hdc in next 7 hdc—8 hdc.

Row 4: Ch 2, turn, sk first st, hdc in next 6 hdc—7 hdc.

Row 5: Ch 2, turn, sk first st, hdc in next 4 hdc, sk next st, sl st in last st. Fasten off.

Left Earflap:
Row 1 (RS): With RS facing, sk 18 sts following right earflap, join E with sl st in next st, ch 2, hdc in next 8 sts; leave rem sts unworked—9 hdc.
Rows 2–5: Work same as rows 2–5 of right earflap. Fasten off.

SIZE 6–12 MONTHS ONLY:
Rnd 5: Ch 2, hdc in same st as joining, hdc in next 3 sts, *2 hdc in next st, hdc in next 3 sts; rep from * around; join with sl st in top of beg ch—45 hdc.
Rnd 6 (RS): With RS facing, join B with sl st in same st as joining, ch 2, hdc in each st around; join with sl st in top of beg ch. Fasten off B.
Rnd 7: With C, rep rnd 6. Fasten off C.
Rnd 8: With D, rep rnd 6.
Rnd 9: Continuing with D, ch 2, hdc in each st around; join with sl st in top of beg ch. Fasten off D.
Rnd 10: With E, rep rnd 6.
Rnd 11: Continuing with E, ch 2, hdc in each st around; join with sl st in top of beg ch. Fasten off E.

Right Earflap:
Row 1 (RS): With RS facing, sk 4 sts following back seam, join E with sl st in next st, ch 2, hdc in next 8 sts; leave rem sts unworked—9 hdc.
Row 2: Ch 2, turn, sk first st, hdc in each st across.
Row 3: Ch 2, turn, sk first st, hdc in next 7 hdc—8 hdc.
Row 4: Ch 2, turn, sk first st, hdc in next 6 hdc—7 hdc.
Row 5: Ch 2, turn, sk first st, hdc in next 4 hdc, sk next st, sl st in last st. Fasten off.

Left Earflap:
Row 1 (RS): With RS facing, sk 21 sts following right earflap, join E with sl st in next st, ch 2, hdc in next 8 sts; leave rem sts unworked—9 hdc.
Rows 2–5: Work same as rows 2–5 of right earflap. Fasten off.

SIZE 12–24 MONTHS ONLY:
Rnd 5: Ch 2, hdc in same st as joining, hdc in next 3 sts, *2 hdc in next st, hdc in next 3 sts; rep from * around; join with sl st in top of beg ch—45 hdc.
Rnd 6: Ch 2, hdc in same st as joining, hdc in next 21 sts, 2 hdc in next st, hdc in each st around; join with sl st in top of beg ch—47 hdc.
Rnd 7 (RS): With RS facing, join B with sl st in same st as joining, ch 2, hdc in each st around; join with sl st in top of beg ch. Fasten off B.
Rnd 8: With C, rep rnd 7. Fasten off C.
Rnd 9: With D, rep rnd 7.
Rnd 10: Continuing with D, ch 2, hdc in each st around; join with sl st in top of beg ch. Fasten off D.
Rnd 11: With E, rep rnd 7.
Rnd 12: Continuing with E, ch 2, hdc in each st around; join with sl st in top of beg ch. Fasten off E.

Right Earflap:
Row 1 (RS): With RS facing, sk 4 sts following back seam, join E with sl st in next st, ch 2, hdc in next 9 sts; leave rem sts unworked—10 hdc.
Rows 2 and 3: Ch 2, turn, sk first st, hdc in each st across.
Row 4: Ch 2, turn, sk first st, hdc in next 8 hdc—9 hdc.
Row 5: Ch 2, turn, sk first st, hdc in next 7 hdc—8 hdc.
Row 6: Ch 2, turn, sk first st, hdc in next 5 hdc, sk next st, sl st in last st. Fasten off.

Left Earflap:

Row 1 (RS): With RS facing, sk 19 sts following right earflap, join E with sl st in next st, ch 2, hdc in next 9 sts; leave rem sts unworked—10 hdc.

Rows 2–6: Work same as rows 2–6 of right earflap. Fasten off.

SIZE 2T–3T ONLY:

Rnd 5: Ch 2, hdc in same st as joining, hdc in next 3 sts, *2 hdc in next st, hdc in next 3 sts; rep from * around; join with sl st in top of beg ch—45 hdc.

Rnd 6: Ch 2, hdc in same st as joining, hdc in next 9 sts, *2 hdc in next st, hdc in next 9 sts; rep from * around to last 5 sts, 2 hdc in next st, hdc in last 4 sts; join with sl st in top of beg ch—50 hdc.

Rnd 7 (RS): With RS facing, join B with sl st in same st as joining, ch 2, hdc in each st around; join with sl st in top of beg ch. Fasten off B.

Rnd 8: With C, rep rnd 7.

Rnd 9: Continuing with C, ch 2, hdc in each st around; join with sl st in top of beg ch. Fasten off C.

Rnd 10: With D, rep rnd 7.

Rnd 11: Continuing with D, ch 2, hdc in each st around; join with sl st in top of beg ch. Fasten off D.

Rnd 12: With E, rep rnd 7.

Rnd 13: Continuing with E, ch 2, hdc in each st around; join with sl st in top of beg ch. Fasten off E.

Right Earflap:

Row 1 (RS): With RS facing, sk 4 sts following back seam, join E with sl st in next st, ch 2, hdc in next 9 sts; leave rem sts unworked—10 hdc.

Rows 2–4: Ch 2, turn, sk first st, hdc in each st across.

Row 5: Ch 2, turn, sk first st, hdc in next 8 hdc—9 hdc.

Row 6: Ch 2, turn, sk first st, hdc in next 7 hdc—8 hdc.

Row 7: Ch 2, turn, sk first st, hdc in next 5 hdc, sk next st, sl st in last st. Fasten off.

Left Earflap:

Row 1 (RS): With RS facing, sk 26 sts following right earflap, join E with sl st in next st, ch 2, hdc in next 9 sts; leave rem sts unworked—10 hdc.

Rows 2–7: Work same as rows 2–7 of right earflap. Fasten off.

ALL SIZES:

Finishing:

With RS facing, join F with sl st in back seam, ch 1, rsc in each st around; join with sl st in beg ch. Fasten off.

Ties (make 2):

With F, ch 2, insert hook under top 2 strands of 2nd ch from hook and draw up a loop, ch 1, yarn over and draw through 2 loops on hook (first foundation sc made), *insert hook under both loops of the chain at the base of the previous foundation sc and draw up a loop, ch 1, yarn over and draw through 2 loops on hook (next foundation sc made); rep from * until Tie is of desired length. Fasten off, leaving a long tail. Use tail to sew tie to tip of one earflap.

Pom-pom:

With F, and following package directions, make a medium size pom-pom and tie pom-pom to top of hat.

Weave in ends.

Boy's Striders

Design by Shehnaaz Afzar

Skill Level: Intermediate

Sizes:

0–3 months (3–6 months, 6–9 months, 9–12 months)

Finished Measurements:

Sole Length: 3½ (3¾, 4¼, 4½) inches/ 9 (9.5, 11, 11.5) cm

Sole Width: 2 (2, 2¼, 2¼) inches/5 (5, 5.5, 5.5) cm

Materials & Tools:

Loops & Threads Impeccable (100% acrylic; 4.5 ounces/128 g = 277 yards/253 m): 1 ball, color aran; OR 1 ball, color grass; OR 1 ball, color true gray—approx 277 yards/253 m of worsted weight yarn (4 MEDIUM)

- **Crochet hook:** 3.75 mm (size F-5 U. S.) or size to obtain gauge
- Sewing needle with matching thread
- 2 wooden buttons, ½ inch/13 mm for the smallest size and ¾ inch/19 mm for the larger sizes.

Gauge:

Use finished sizes of soles for gauge. Always take time to check your gauge.

Stitches:

chain (ch)

single crochet (sc)

slip stitch (sl st)

half double crochet (hdc)

half double crochet 2 together (hdc2tog)

single crochet 2 together (sc2tog)

double crochet 3 together (dc3tog)

Notes:

1. The beauty of your shoe depends on the width and breadth of your strap, so customize it to your taste. If you want it to be longer, add 1 or 2 chains and follow the same pattern. If you want it to be longer as well as wider, switch to a larger hook.

2. One ball of the specified yarn will make multiple pairs of booties.

3. At end of each rnd when pattern says "join with sl st in beg ch-1," sl st in the next stitch visible. When it says "join with sl st in first sc," skip the beginning ch-1 (next stitch visible) and sl st in the next stitch (the first sc).

INSTRUCTIONS

BOOTIES (MAKE 2):

Sole:

Sizes 0–3 months (3–6 months) ONLY:

Ch 10 (12).

Rnd 1 (RS): Sc in 2nd ch from hook and in each ch across to last ch, 3 sc in last ch; rotate piece (but do not turn) to work across opposite side of foundation ch, sc in each ch across to last ch, 2 sc in last ch; join with sl st in beg ch-1—20 (24) sc.

Rnd 2: Ch 1, 2 sc in next st, sc in next 3 (4) sts, hdc in next 4 (5) sts, 2 hdc in each of next 3 sts, hdc in next 4 (5) sts, sc in next 3 (4) sts, 2 sc in each of last 2 sts; join with sl st in beg ch-1—26 (30) sts.

Rnd 3: Ch 1, sc in next st, 2 sc in next st, sc in next 8 (10) sts, 2 sc in next st, sc in next 4 sts, 2 sc in next st, sc in next 8 (10) sts, 2 sc in next st, sc in last st; join with sl st in beg ch-1—30 (34) sc.

Rnd 4: Ch 1, sc in next 2 sts, 2 sc in next st, sc in next 5 (6) sts, hdc in next 4 (5) sts, 2 hdc in each of next 2 sts, hdc in next 2 sts, 2 hdc in each of next 2 sts, hdc in next 4 (5) sts, sc in next 5 (6) sts, 2 sc in next st, sc in last 2 sts; join with sl st in first sc—36 (40) sts. Do not fasten off.

Sizes 6–9 months (9–12 months) ONLY:
Ch 13 (14). Ch uniformly to maintain gauge and keep your sole stiff.
Rnd 1: Sc in 2nd ch from hook, sc in next 6 (7) ch, hdc in next 4 ch, 3 hdc in last ch; rotate piece (but do not turn) to work across opposite side of foundation ch, hdc in next 4 ch, sc in next 6 (7) ch, 2 sc in last ch; join with sl st in beg ch-1—26 (28) sc.
Rnd 2: Ch 1, 2 sc in next st, sc in next 5 (6) sts, hdc in next 5 sts, 2 hdc in each of next 4 sts, hdc in next 5 sts, sc in next 5 (6) sts, 3 sc in last st; join with sl st in beg ch-1—33 (35) sts.
Rnd 3: Ch 1, sc in next st, 2 sc in next st, sc in next 12 (13) sts, 2 sc in next st, sc in next 3 sts, 2 sc in next st, sc in next 12 (13) sts, 2 sc in last 2 sts; join with sl st in beg ch-1—38 (40) sts.
Rnd 4: Ch 1, sc in next 10 (11) sts, hdc in next 5 sts, 2 hdc in each of next 2 sts, hdc in next 3 sts, 2 hdc in each of next 2 sts, hdc in next 5 sts, sc in next 10 (11) sts, 2 sc in last st; join with sl st in first sc—43 (45) sts. Do not fasten off.

Sides:
Size 0–3 months ONLY:
Rnd 1 (RS): Ch 2 (does not count as a st), working in BL only, hdc in next st, hdc in each st around, working last hdc in st at base of beg ch-2; join with sl st in first hdc.

Rnd 2: Do not turn. Working in both loops, ch 1 (does not count as a st), sc in next hdc, sc in each hdc around working last sc in st at base of beg ch-1; join with sl st in first sc. Do not fasten off.

Size 3–6 months ONLY:
Rnd 1 (RS): Ch 2 (does not count as a st), working in BL only, hdc in next st, hdc in each st around, working last hdc in st at base of beg ch-2; join with sl st in first hdc.
Rnd 2: Ch 2, working in both loops, hdc in next st, hdc in each st around, working last hdc in st at base of beg ch-2; join with sl st in first hdc. Do not fasten off.

Sizes 6–9 months (9–12 months) ONLY:
Rnd 1 (RS): Ch 1 (does not count as a st), working in BL only, sc in next st, sc in each st around, working last sc in st at base of beg ch-1; join with sl st in first sc.
Rnd 2: Working in both loops, ch 2 (does not count as a st), hdc in next st, hdc in each st around, working last hdc in st at base of beg ch-2; join with sl st in first hdc.
Rnd 3: Ch 1, sc in next st, sc in each st around, working last sc in st at base of beg ch-1; join with sl st in first sc. Do not fasten off.

Toe Top Notes:
1. Before you start the toe top rounds, make sure the right side of the sole is under the shoe with a round of free loops running around it. If not, just flip the sides to ensure your toe top will be worked on the correct side.

2. Markers are placed to indicate the stitches at the toe end (wide end) of the bootie.
3. When working the first round of the Toe Top, you will work in the BL only when working in the stitches between the markers.
4. "Move marker up" means after you work a stitch in a marked stitch, take the marker out and place it in the new stitch you worked into the marked stitch.
5. Following the markers in the pattern will ensure that your work doesn't get lopsided.
6. To mark a stitch, you just have to pull a piece of contrasting color yarn through it.
7. Identify the 18 (20, 24, 26) stitches centered over the toe end (wide end) of bootie, and place a marker in the first and last of these stitches.

Sizes 0–3 months (3–6 months) ONLY:
Rnd 1: Ch 2, hdc in next st, hdc in each st to 4 sts before first marker, hdc2tog, hdc in next 2 sts; working in BL only, hdc in marked st and move marker up, hdc in next 2 (3) sts, hdc2tog twice, hdc in next st, hdc2tog, hdc in next st, hdc2tog twice, hdc in next 2 (3) sts, hdc in marked st and move marker up; working in both loops, hdc in next 2 sts, hdc2tog, hdc in each st around working last hdc in st at base of beg ch-2; join with sl st in first hdc—29 (33) sts.
Note: There should be 13 (15) sts between the markers (including the marked sts) centered over toe end of bootie.
Rnd 2: Ch 1, do not turn, working in both loops, sc in next st, sc in each st to first marker, hdc in marked st and move marker up, hdc in next 3 (4) sts, hdc2tog, hdc in next st, hdc2tog, hdc in next 3 (4) sts, hdc in marked st and move marker up, sc in each sc around, working last sc in st at base of beg ch-1; join with sl st in first sc—27 (31) sts.
Notes: There should be 11 (13) sts between the markers (including the marked sts). The piece may look a little asymmetrical, but that is fine. When instructed to work into "0" sts this means you should skip that part of the instruction and proceed with the next part of the instruction.
Rnd 3: Ch 1, sc in next st, sc in each st to first marker, hdc in marked st and remove marker, hdc in next 0 (1) st, hdc2tog twice, hdc in next st, hdc2tog twice, hdc in next 0 (1) st, hdc in marked st and remove marker, sc in each st around, working last sc in st at base of beg ch-1—23 (27) sts.

Size 0–3 months ONLY:
Rnd 4: Keeping your sl sts loose, sl st in next st, sc2tog, [sc in next st, sk next st] 4 times, sc in next st, sc2tog, sl st in each st around; join with sl st in first sl st—17 sts. Fasten off.

Size 3–6 months ONLY:
Rnd 4: Sl st in next 3 sts, sc2tog, hdc2tog twice, hdc in next st, hdc2tog twice, sc2tog, sl st in each remaining st around; join with sl st in first sl st—21 sts. Fasten off.

Sizes 6–9 months (9–12 months) ONLY:
Rnd 1: Ch 2, hdc in next st, hdc in each st to 4 sts before first marker, hdc2tog, hdc in next 2 sts; working in BL only, hdc in marked st and move marker up, hdc in next 5 (6) sts, hdc2tog twice, hdc in next st, hdc2tog, hdc in next st, hdc2tog twice, hdc in next 5 (6) sts, hdc in marked st and move marker up; working in both loops, hdc in

next 2 sts, hdc2tog, hdc in each st around working last hdc in st at base of beg ch-2—36 (38) sts.
Note: There should be 19 (21) sts between the markers (including the marked sts) centered over toe end of bootie.
Rnd 2: Ch 1, do not turn, working in both loops, sc in next st, sc in each st to first marker, hdc in marked st and move marker up, hdc in next 6 (7) sts, hdc2tog, hdc in next st, hdc2tog, hdc in next 6 (7) sts, hdc in marked st and move marker up, sc in each sc around, working last sc in st at base of beg ch-1—34 (36) sts.
Notes: There should be 17 (19) sts between the markers (including the marked sts). The piece may look a little asymmetrical, but that is fine.
Rnd 3: Ch 1, sc in next st, sc in each st to first marker, hdc in marked st and remove marker, hdc in next 1 (2) sts, [hdc2tog] 3 times, hdc in next st, [hdc2tog] 3 times, hdc in next 1 (2) sts, hdc in marked st and remove marker, sc in each st around, working last sc in st at base of beg ch-1—28 (30) sts.
Rnd 4: Keeping your sl sts loose, sl st in next 4 (5) sts, sc in next st, hdc in next 2 sts, hdc2tog, dc3tog, hdc2tog, hdc in next 2 sts, sc in next st, sl st in each st around; join with sl st in first sl st—24 (26) sts. Fasten off.

Straps:
Sizes 0–3 months (3–6 months) ONLY:
Ch 12 (13).
Rnd 1: Hdc in 4th ch from hook (skipped chains form the buttonhole), hdc in next ch, sl st in next 5 (6) ch, hdc in next ch, (hdc, ch 2, hdc) in last ch (the ch-2 just made forms the second buttonhole); working across opposite side of foundation ch,

hdc in next ch, sl st in next 5 (6) ch, hdc in next 2 ch; join with sl st in next ch—8 hdc, 10 (12) sl sts and a ch-2 buttonhole at each end of piece.
Rnd 2: Ch 1, 4 sc in first ch-2 sp, 2 sc in next st, sc in next st, sl st in BL only of next 5 (6) sts, sc in next st, 2 sc in next st, 4 sc in next ch-2 sp, 2 sc in next st, sc in next st, sl st in BL only of next 5 (6) sts, sc in next st, 2 sc in next st; join with sl st in first sc. Fasten off.

Sizes 6–9 months (9–12 months) ONLY:
Ch 14.
Rnd 1: Hdc in 4th ch from hook (skipped chains form buttonhole), hdc in next ch, sl st in next 7 ch, hdc in next ch, (hdc, ch 2, hdc) in last ch (the ch-2 just made forms the second buttonhole); working across opposite side of foundation ch, hdc in next ch, sl st in next 7 ch, hdc in next 2 ch; join with sl st in next ch—8 hdc, 14 sl sts, and a ch-2 buttonhole at each end of piece.
Rnd 2: Ch 1, 4 hdc in first ch-2 sp, 2 hdc in next st, sc in next st, sl st in BL only of next 7 sts, sc in next st, 2 hdc in next st, 4 hdc in next ch-2 sp, 2 hdc in next st, sc in next st, sl st in BL only of next 7 sts, sc in next sts, 2 hdc in next st; join with sl st in first hdc. Fasten off.

FINISHING:
Weave in ends.
Sew one button to one side of instep, and button on one end of strap. Place strap across instep of bootie and mark for placement of second button, making sure that the buttons are symmetrically placed. Sew second button in place.

High Country Booties

Design by Julie Barber

Skill Level: Easy

Sizes:

0–3 months (3–6 months, 6–9 months, 9–12 months)

Finished Measurements:

Sole Length: 3¾ (4, 4¼, 4¾) inches/ 9.5 (10, 11, 12) cm

Materials & Tools:

Lily Sugar 'n Cream (100% cotton; 2.5 ounces/71 g = 120 yards/109 m): 1 ball, color of your choice—approx 120 yards/109 m of worsted weight yarn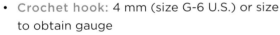

- Crochet hook: 4 mm (size G-6 U.S.) or size to obtain gauge
- Yarn needle

Gauge:

6 hdc and 5 rows = 1¾ inches/4.5 cm
Always take time to check your gauge.

Stitches:

chain (ch)
slip stitch (sl st)
half double crochet (hdc)
double crochet (dc)
double crochet 2 together (dc2tog)
half double crochet 2 together (hdc2tog)
single crochet (sc)
back post double crochet (BPdc)*
front post double crochet (FPdc)*
double crochet 6 together (dc6tog)*

*SPECIAL STITCHES

Back Post double crochet (BPdc): Yarn over, insert hook from back to front to back again around post of indicated stitch, yarn over and draw up a loop, [yarn over and draw through 2 loops on hook] twice.

Front Post double crochet (FPdc): Yarn over, insert hook from front to back to front again around post of indicated stitch, yarn over and draw up a loop, [yarn over and draw through 2 loops on hook] twice.

Double crochet 6 together (dc6tog): *Yarn over, insert hook in next stitch, yarn over and draw up a loop, yarn over and draw through 2 loops on hook; rep from * 5 more times, yarn over and draw through all 7 loops on hook.

Invisible stitch (for joining final rounds): Cut working yarn leaving a long tail. Yarn over with tail and draw all the way through loop on hook and tighten to form a knot. Thread tail onto yarn needle and take under top two loops of first stitch of round, then back down through center of last stitch of round and to the wrong/inside of the piece. Weave in ends securely on the wrong side of piece.

INSTRUCTIONS

SIZE 0–3 MONTHS ONLY (make 2):
Ch 11.

Sole:
Rnd 1 (RS): Work 3 hdc in 2nd ch from hook, hdc in next 8 ch, 5 hdc in last ch; working across opposite side of foundation ch, hdc in next 8 ch; join with sl st in beg ch-1 (the skipped ch)—24 sts.
Rnd 2: Ch 1, 2 hdc in each of first 3 sts, hdc in next 5 sts, dc in next 3 sts, 2 dc in each of next 5 sts, dc in next 3 sts, hdc in last 5 sts; join with sl st in beg ch-1—32 sts.

Shape Sides and Top:
Rnd 3: Working in BL only, ch 1, hdc in first 15 sts, dc in next 10 sts, hdc in last 7 sts; join with sl st in beg ch-1.
Rnd 4: Working in both loops, ch 1, hdc in first 11 sts, [dc2tog] 8 times, hdc in last 5 sts; join with sl st in beg ch-1—24 sts.
Rnd 5: Ch 1, hdc in first 11 sts, [hdc2tog, hdc next st] 3 times, hdc in last 4 sts; join with sl st in beg ch-1—21 sts.
Rnd 6: Ch 1, sc in each st around; join with sl st in beg ch-1.
Rnd 7: Ch 2, dc in each st around; join with sl st in top of beg ch-2.

Ribbed Cuff:
Rnd 8: Ch 2, FPdc around first dc, *BPdc around next dc, FPdc around next dc; rep from * around; join with sl st in top of beg ch-2.
Rnds 9 and 10: Ch 2, FPdc around first FPdc, *BPdc around next BPdc, FPdc around next FPdc; rep from * around; join with sl st in top of beg ch-2.

Rnd 11: Ch 1, hdc in each st around; join with invisible st * in first hdc.
Fasten off.

SIZE 3–6 MONTHS ONLY (make 2):
Ch 9.

Sole:
Rnd 1 (RS): Work 3 hdc in 2nd ch from hook, hdc in next 6 ch, 5 hdc in last ch; working across opposite side of foundation ch, hdc in next 6 ch; join with sl st in beg ch-1 (the skipped ch)—20 sts.
Rnd 2: Ch 1, 2 hdc in each of first 3 sts, sc in next 5 sts, hdc in next st, 2 hdc in each of next 5 sts, hdc in next st, sc in last 5 sts; join with sl st in beg ch-1—28 sts.
Rnd 3: Ch 1, [2 hdc in next st, hdc next st] 3 times, hdc in next 6 sts, [2 hdc in next st, hdc next st] 5 times, hdc in last 6 sts; join with sl st in beg ch-1—36 sts.

Shape Sides and Top:
Rnd 4: Working in BL only, ch 1, sc in first 16 sts, hdc in next 16 sts, sc in last 4 sts; join with sl st in beg ch-1.
Rnd 5: Working in both loops, ch 1, sc in first 15 sts, hdc in next 18 sts, sc in last 3 sts; join with sl st in beg ch-1.
Rnd 6: Ch 1, hdc in first 15 sts, [dc2tog] 9 times, hdc in last 3 sts; join with sl st in beg ch-1—27 sts.
Rnd 7: Ch 1, hdc in first 13 sts, [hdc2tog] 7 times; join with sl st in beg ch-1—20 sts.
Rnd 8: Ch 1, sc in each st around; join with sl st in beg ch-1.
Rnd 9: Ch 2, dc in first 17 sts, 2 dc in next st, dc in last 2 sts; join with sl st in beg ch-1—21 sts.

Sole:

Rnd 1 (RS): Work 3 hdc in 2nd ch from hook, hdc in next 8 ch, 5 hdc in last ch; working across opposite side of foundation ch, hdc in next 8 ch; join with sl st in beg ch-1 (the skipped ch)—24 sts.
Rnd 2: Ch 1, 2 sc in each of first 3 sts, sc in next 6 sts, hdc in next 2 sts, 2 hdc in each of next 5 sts, hdc in next 2 sts, sc in last 6 sts; join with sl st in beg ch-1—32 sts.
Rnd 3: Ch 1, [2 hdc in next st, hdc next st] 3 times, hdc in next 8 sts, [2 hdc in next st, hdc next st] 5 times, hdc in last 8 sts; join with sl st in beg ch-1—40 sts.

Shape Sides and Top:

Rnd 4: Working in BL only, ch 1, sc in first 18 sts, hdc in next 16 sts, sc in last 6 sts; join with sl st in beg ch-1.
Rnd 5: Working in both loops, ch 1, sc in first 17 sts, hdc in next 18 sts, sc in last 5 sts; join with sl st in beg ch-1.
Rnd 6: Ch 1, hdc in first 17 sts, [dc2tog] 9 times, hdc in last 5 sts; join with sl st in beg ch-1—31 sts.
Rnd 7: Ch 1, hdc in first 15 sts, [hdc2tog] 7 times, hdc in last 2 sts; join with sl st in beg ch-1—24 sts.
Rnd 8: Ch 1, sc in first 15 sts, [sc2tog, sc in next st] 3 times; join with sl st in beg ch-1—21 sts.
Rnd 9: Ch 2, dc in each st around; join with sl st in top of beg ch-2.

Ribbed Cuff:

Rnd 10: Ch 2, FPdc around first dc, *BPdc around next dc, FPdc around next dc; rep from * around; join with sl st in top of beg ch-2.
Rnds 11–14: Ch 2, FPdc around first FPdc, *BPdc around next BPdc, FPdc around next FPdc; rep from * around; join with sl st in top of beg ch-2.

Ribbed Cuff:

Rnd 10: Ch 2, FPdc around first dc, *BPdc around next dc, FPdc around next dc; rep from * around; join with sl st in top of beg ch-2.
Rnds 11–13: Ch 2, FPdc around first FPdc, *BPdc around next BPdc, FPdc around next FPdc; rep from * around; join with sl st in top of beg ch-2.
Rnd 14: Ch 1, hdc in each st around; join with invisible st in first hdc.
Fasten off.

SIZE 6–9 MONTHS ONLY (make 2):
Ch 11.

Rnd 15: Ch 1, hdc in each st around; join with invisible st in first hdc.
Fasten off.

SIZE 9–12 MONTHS ONLY (Make 2):
Ch 13.

Sole:
Rnd 1 (RS): Work 3 hdc in 2nd ch from hook, hdc in next 10 ch, 5 hdc in last ch; working across opposite side of foundation ch, hdc in next 10 ch; join with sl st in beg ch-1 (the skipped ch)—28 sts.
Rnd 2: Ch 1, 2 sc in each of first 3 sts, sc in next 6 sts, hdc in next 4 sts, 2 hdc in each of next 5 sts, hdc in next 4 sts, sc in last 6 sts; join with sl st in beg ch-1—36 sts.
Rnd 3: Ch 1, [2 hdc in next st, hdc next st] 3 times, hdc in next 10 sts, [2 hdc in next st, hdc next st] 5 times, hdc in last 10 sts; join with sl st in beg ch-1—44 sts.

Shape Sides and Top:
Rnd 4: Working in BL only, ch 1, sc in first 20 sts, hdc in next 16 sts, sc in last 8 sts; join with sl st in beg ch-1.
Rnd 5: Working in both loops, ch 1, sc in first 19 sts, hdc in next 18 sts, sc in last 7 sts; join with sl st in beg ch-1.
Rnd 6: Ch 1, hdc in first 19 sts, [dc2tog] 9 times, hdc in last 7 sts; join with sl st in beg ch-1—35 sts.
Rnd 7: Ch 1, hdc in first 17 sts, [hdc2tog] 7 times, hdc in last 4 sts; join with sl st in beg ch-1—28 sts.
Rnd 8: Ch 1, sc in first 18 sts, dc6tog, sc in last 4 sts; join with sl st in beg ch-1—23 sts.

Rnd 9: Ch 2, dc in each st around; join with sl st in top of beg ch-2.

Ribbed Cuff:
Rnd 10: Ch 2, FPdc around first dc, *BPdc around next dc, FPdc around next dc; rep from * around; join with sl st in top of beg ch-2.
Rnds 11–15: Ch 2, FPdc around first FPdc, *BPdc around next BPdc, FPdc around next FPdc; rep from * around; join with sl st in top of beg ch-2.
Rnd 16: Ch 1, hdc in each st around; join with invisible st in first hdc.
Fasten off.

FINISHING:
Weave in any remaining ends.

Plain Janes

Design by Julie Barber

Skill Level: Easy

Sizes:

0–3 months (3–6 months, 6–9 months, 9–12 months)

Finished Measurements

Sole Length: 3¾ (4, 4¼, 4¾) inches/9.5 (10, 11, 12) cm

Materials and Tools:

Lily Sugar 'n Cream (100% cotton; 2.5 ounces/71 g = 120 yards/109 m): (A), 1 ball, color white #00001; (B), 1 ball, color soft violet #00093; (C), 1 ball, color sage green #00084—approx 260 yards/238 m of worsted weight yarn ④ MEDIUM

Note: You will not need a whole ball of each color.

- Crochet hooks: 3.25 mm (size D-3 U.S.) and 3.5 mm (size E-4 U.S.) or size to obtain gauge
- Yarn Needle
- 2 buttons, ½ inch/13 mm diameter

Gauge:

6 hdc and 5 rows = 1½ inches/4 cm, with larger hook.

Always take time to check your gauge.

Stitches:

- chain (ch)
- half double crochet (hdc)
- double crochet (dc)
- slip stitch (sl st)
- single crochet (sc)
- half double crochet 2 together (hdc2tog)

- single crochet 2 together (sc2tog)
- double crochet 2 together (dc2tog)
- treble crochet (tr)

SPECIAL STITCH

Invisible stitch (for joining final rounds): Cut working yarn leaving a long tail. Yarn over with tail and draw all the way through loop on hook and tighten to form a knot. Thread tail onto yarn needle and take under top two loops of first stitch of round, then back down through center of last stitch of round and to the wrong/inside of the piece. Weave in ends securely on the wrong side of piece.

Notes:

1. Larger hook is used to make slippers. Smaller hook is used to make leaf and flower embellishment. For larger leaf and flowers, use larger hook.
2. Only a small amount of yarn (C) is used for the leaves.
3. One ball of each color yarn will make multiple pairs of slippers.

INSTRUCTIONS

SIZE 0–3 MONTHS ONLY (make 2):
With larger hook and A, ch 10.

Sole:

Rnd 1 (RS): Work 3 hdc in 2nd ch from hook, hdc in next 4 ch, dc in next 3 ch, 6 dc in last ch; working across opposite side of foundation ch, dc in next 3 ch, hdc in last 4 ch; join with sl st in beg ch-1 (the skipped ch)—23 sts.
Rnd 2: Ch 1, 2 sc in each of first 3 sts, sc in next 4 sts, hdc in next 3 sts, 2 hdc in each of next 6 sts, hdc next 3 sts, sc in last 4 sts; join with sl st in beg ch-1—32 sts.
Rnd 3: Ch 1, [2 sc in next st, sc in next st] 3 times, sc in next 3 sts, hdc in next 4 sts, [2 hdc in next st, hdc in next st] 6 times, hdc in next 4 sts, sc in last 3 sts; join with sl st in beg ch-1—41 sts. Fasten off.

Sides and Top:

Rnd 4: With RS facing, draw up a loop of B in joining sl st; working in BL only, ch 1, hdc in first 16 sts, dc in next 18 sts, hdc in last 7 sts; join with sl st in beg ch-1.

Rnd 5: Working in both loops, ch 1, hdc in first 16 sts, [hdc2tog, hdc in next st] 6 times, hdc in last 7 sts; join with sl st in beg ch-1—35 sts.
Rnd 6: Ch 1, hdc in first 12 sts, sc next 3 sts, [sc2tog, sc in next st] 6 times, sc in last 2 sts; join with sl st in beg ch-1—29 sts.
Rnd 7: Ch 1, sc in first 3 sts, hdc in next 6 sts, sc in next 6 sts, [hdc2tog] 6 times, sc in last 2 sts; join with sl st in first sc—23 sts.

Strap:

Rnd 8: Sl st in next 12 sts (Left Slipper) or 22 sts (Right Slipper), ch 12, sc in 6th ch from hook and next 6 ch, sl st in next st of previous rnd of slipper and in each st to end of round; join with invisible st* in first sl st (Left Slipper), or join with invisible st in first sl st and sl st in next st (Right Slipper). Fasten off.

SIZE 3–6 MONTHS ONLY (make 2):
With larger hook and A, ch 11.

Sole:

Rnd 1 (RS): Work 3 hdc in 2nd ch from hook, hdc in next 5 ch, dc in next 3 ch, 6 dc in last ch; working across opposite side of foundation ch, dc in next 3 ch, hdc in last 5 ch; join with sl st in beg ch-1 (the skipped ch)—25 sts.
Rnd 2: Ch 1, 2 sc in each of first 3 sts, sc in next 4 sts, hdc in next 4 sts, 2 hdc in each of next 6 sts, hdc next 4 sts, sc in last 4 sts; join with sl st in beg ch-1—34 sts.
Rnd 3: Ch 1, [2 sc in next st, sc in next st] 3 times, hdc in next 8 sts, [2 hdc in next st, hdc in next st] 6 times, hdc in last 8 sts; join with sl st in beg ch-1—43 sts. Fasten off.

Sides and Top:

Rnd 4: With RS facing, draw up a loop of B in joining sl st; working in BL only, ch 1, dc in first 9 sts, hdc in next 9 sts, dc in next 18 sts, hdc in last 7 sts; join with sl st in beg ch-1.

Rnd 5: Working in both loops, ch 1, hdc in first 18 sts, [hdc2tog, hdc in next st] 6 times, hdc in last 7 sts; join with sl st in beg ch-1—37 sts.

Rnd 6: Ch 1, sc in first 14 sts, [sc2tog, sc in next st] 6 times, sc in last 5 sts; join with sl st in beg ch-1—31 sts.

Rnd 7: Ch 1, sc in first 3 sts, hdc in next 6 sts, sc in next 6 sts, [hdc2tog] 6 times, sc in last 4 sts; join with sl st in first sc—25 sts.

Strap:

Rnd 8: Sl st in next 13 sts (Left Slipper) or 23 sts (Right Slipper), ch 12, sc in 6th ch from hook and next 6 ch, sl st in next st of previous rnd of slipper and in each st to end of round; join with invisible st * in first sl st.
Fasten off.

SIZE 6–9 MONTHS ONLY (make 2):
With larger hook and A, ch 12.

Sole:

Rnd 1 (RS): Work 3 hdc in 2nd ch from hook, hdc in next 6 ch, dc in next 3 ch, 6 dc in last ch; working across opposite side of foundation ch, dc in next 3 ch, hdc in last 6 ch; join with sl st in beg ch-1 (the skipped ch)—27 sts.

Rnd 2: Ch 1, 2 hdc in each of first 3 sts, hdc in next 6 sts, dc in next 3 sts, 2 dc in each of next 6 sts, dc next 3 sts, hdc in last 6 sts; join with sl st in beg ch-1—36 sts.

Rnd 3: Ch 1, [2 hdc in next st, hdc in next st] 3 times, hdc in next 9 sts, [2 hdc in next st, hdc in next st] 6 times, hdc in last 9 sts; join with sl st in beg ch-1—45 sts. Fasten off.

Sides and Top:

Rnd 4: With RS facing, draw up a loop of B in joining sl st; working in BL only, ch 1, dc in first 12 sts, hdc in next 6 sts, dc in next 20 sts, hdc in next 6 sts, dc in last st; join with sl st in beg ch-1.

Rnd 5: Working in both loops, ch 1, hdc in first 17 sts, dc in next 2 sts, [dc2tog, dc in next st] 6 times, dc in next st, hdc in last 7 sts; join with sl st in beg ch-1—39 sts.

Rnd 6: Ch 1, hdc in first 15 sts, sc in next 3 sts, [sc2tog, sc in next st] 6 times, sc in next 2 sts, hdc in last st; join with sl st in beg ch-1—33 sts.

Rnd 7: Ch 1, hdc in first 3 sts, dc in next 9 sts, hdc in next 7 sts, [dc2tog] 6 times, hdc in last 2 sts; join with sl st in first hdc—27 sts.

Strap:

Rnd 8: Sl st in next 15 sts (Left Slipper) or 25 sts (Right Slipper), ch 12, sc in 6th ch from hook and next 6 ch, sl st in next st of previous rnd of slipper and in each st to end of round; join with invisible st* in first sl st.
Fasten off.

SIZE 9–12 MONTHS ONLY (make 2):
With larger hook and A, ch 14.

Sole:

Rnd 1 (RS): Work 3 hdc in 2nd ch from hook, hdc in next 7 ch, dc in next 4 ch, 6 dc in last ch;

working across opposite side of foundation ch, dc in next 4 ch, hdc in last 7 ch; join with sl st in beg ch-1 (the skipped ch)—31 sts.

Rnd 2: Ch 1, 2 hdc in each of first 3 sts, hdc in next 8 sts, dc in next 3 sts, 2 dc in each of next 6 sts, dc next 3 sts, hdc in last 8 sts; join with sl st in beg ch-1—40 sts.

Rnd 3: Ch 1, [2 hdc in next st, hdc in next st] 3 times, hdc in next 11 sts, [2 hdc in next st, hdc in next st] 6 times, hdc in last 11 sts; join with sl st in beg ch-1—49 sts. Fasten off.

Sides and Top:

Rnd 4: With RS facing, draw up a loop of B in joining sl st; working in BL only, ch 1, dc in first 12 sts, hdc in next 8 sts, dc in next 20 sts, hdc in next 8 sts, dc in last st; join with sl st in beg ch-1.

Rnd 5: Working in both loops, ch 1, hdc in first 20 sts, dc in next 2 sts, [dc2tog, dc in next st] 6 times, dc in next st, hdc in last 8 sts; join with sl st in beg ch-1—43 sts.

Rnd 6: Ch 1, hdc first 16 sts, sc in next 3 sts, [sc2tog, sc in next st] 6 times, sc in next 2 sts, hdc in last 4 sts; join with sl st in beg ch-1—37 sts.

Rnd 7: Ch 1, hdc in first 3 sts, dc in next 9 sts, hdc in next 8 sts, [dc2tog] 6 times, hdc in last 5 sts; join with sl st in first hdc—31 sts.

Strap:

Rnd 8: Sl st in next 16 sts (Left Slipper) or 26 sts (Right Slipper), ch 12, sc in 6th ch from hook and next 6 ch, sl st in next st of previous rnd of slipper and in each st to end of round; join with invisible st in first sl st.
Fasten off.

ALL SIZES:

Three-Petal Flower (make 2):

With smaller hook and A, ch 3.

Rnd 1: Sl st in 3rd ch from hook, *(ch 2, 2 tr in same ch, ch 2, sl st) in same ch; rep from * 2 more times.
Fasten off, leaving a long tail for sewing. Pull tail through center of flower to bring it to the back of the flower.

Leaf (make 2):

With smaller hook and C, ch 10.

Rnd 1: Sl st in 2nd ch from hook, sl st in next ch, sc in next ch, hdc in next ch, dc in next 2 ch, tr in next 2 ch, (tr, 3 sc, tr) in last ch; working across opposite side of foundation ch, tr in next 2 ch, dc in next 2 ch, hdc in next ch, sc in next ch, sl st in next ch; join with sl st in beg ch-1 (skipped ch).
Fasten off, leaving a long tail for sewing.

FINISHING:

Sew one button to each slipper opposite the beginning end of the strap. Place one flower on top of each leaf and sew in place. Sew one flower and leaf pair to each slipper, sewing piece slightly below button. Weave in any remaining ends.

High Tops

Design by Debbie Roney

Skill Level: Intermediate

Sizes:
0–3 months (3–6 months)

Finished Measurements:
Sole Length 3½ (4) inches/9 (10) cm

Materials & Tools:
Red Heart Super Saver (100% acrylic; 7 ounces/198 g = 364 yards/333 m): (A), 1 skein, color white #0311; (B), 1 skein, color spring green #0672; (C), 2 yards/2 m, color paddy green #0368—approx 728 yards/666 m of worsted weight yarn [4] MEDIUM
Note: You will not need a whole skein of each color.

- Crochet hook: 3.75 mm (size F-5 U.S.) or size to obtain gauge
- Stitch marker
- Yarn needle

Gauge:
Use finished length of soles for gauge. Always take time to check your gauge.

Stitches:
chain (ch)
slip stitch (sl st)
double crochet (dc)
half double crochet (hdc)
single crochet (sc)
double crochet 2 together (dc2tog)
single crochet 2 together (sc2tog)

INSTRUCTIONS

HIGH TOP (MAKE 2):

Sole:
With A, ch 12 (14).
Rnd 1: Sc in 2nd ch from hook, sc in next 6 (8) ch, hdc in next 2 ch, 2 hdc in next ch, 5 hdc in last ch; working across opposite side of foundation ch, 2 hdc in next ch, hdc in next 2 ch, sc in next 6 (8) ch, 2 sc in next ch; do not join, work in continuous rnds—28 (32) sts. Place marker in last stitch to indicate end of round. Move marker up as each round is completed.
Rnd 2: 2 sc in next st, sc in next 10 (12) sts, [2 sc in next st, sc in next st] 3 times, sc in next 9 (11) sts, 2 sc in next st, sc in next st—33 (37) sts.
Rnd 3: 2 sc in next st, sc in next 11 (13) sts, [2 sc in next st, sc in next st] twice, [sc in next st, 2 sc in next st] twice, sc in next 11 (13) sts, 2 sc in next st, sc in next st; join with sl st in next st—39 (43) sts.

Shape Sides:
Rnd 4: Working in BL only, ch 1, sc in each sc around; join with sl st in beg ch-1.
Rnd 5: Working in both loops, ch 1, sc in each sc around; join with sl st in beg ch-1. Fasten off.

Stripe:
Thread a length of C onto yarn needle and backstitch a line around the sides of the sole, between rnds 4 and 5. Tie ends of back stitch line together, and carefully hide and trim end.

Toe:

Row 1 (RS): Fold sole in half along the foundation chain. From RS, draw up a loop of A in the 5th st from the center of the toe end (wide end), ch 1, sk next sc, dc in next 2 sc, dc2tog, dc in next 2 sc, sk next sc, sl st in next sc. Fasten off A, leaving a long enough tail to ensure that this row does not unravel as you work the tongue.

Tongue:

With RS facing, draw up a loop of B in BL of first sl st of toe.

Row 1 (RS): Working in BL only, ch 1, sc in same sl st, sc in rem 6 sts of toe—7 sc.

Rows 2–4: Ch 1, turn, sc in each sc across.

Row 5: Ch 1, turn, sk first sc, sc last 6 sc.

Row 6: Ch 1, turn, sk first sc, sc in last 5 sc.

Rows 7–12: Ch 1, turn, sc in each sc across.

Row 13: Ch 3 (counts as dc), turn, sk first sc, dc in last 4 sc—5 dc.

Fasten off. Weave in end by weaving it through the top of the last row. You will need the posts of the stitches of the last row free to lace the shoe; take care not to weave the end through the posts.

Sides:

With RS facing, join B with sl st in BL of first st of side of sole following toe.

Row 1 (RS): Ch 1, sc in each unworked st of last rnd of sole—29 (33) sc.

Row 2: Ch 1, turn, sc in each sc across.

Row 3: Ch 1, turn, sk first sc, sc in next 26 (30) sc, sc2tog—27 (31) sc.

Row 4: Ch 1, turn, sk first sc, sc in next sc, sc2tog, sc in next 19 (23) sc, [sc2tog] twice—23 (27) sts.

Row 5: Ch 1, turn, sk first sc, sc in next sc, sc2tog, sc in next 15 (19) sc, [sc2tog] twice—19 (23) sts.

Rows 6–10: Ch 1, turn, sc in each st across. Fasten off.

Top Edge:

Row 1 (RS): With RS facing, join A with sl st in first st of last row, sl st in each rem st across. Fasten off.

LACES (MAKE 2):

With A and leaving a 2-inch-long/5 cm beg tail, ch 105. Fasten off, leaving a tail about 2 inches/ 5 cm long.

CIRCLES (MAKE 4):

With A, make an adjustable ring.

Rnd 1: Ch 1, 7 sc in ring; join with sl st in first sc. Fasten off, leaving a long tail for sewing circle to high top. Pull beg tail to close center opening. Weave in and trim beg tail.

FINISHING:

Using photograph as a guide to placement, with long yarn tail, sew one circle to each side of ankle of each high top.

Thread the laces through the spaces between stitches up the front of the sides, as if lacing a shoe. At the top, thread each end of the lace around the 2nd post from the edge of the top of the tongue and then through the front edge of the shoe. Tie the ends in a bow. Cut ends ¼ inch/6 mm long, to simulate the aglet at the tip of regular shoe laces.

Weave in any remaining ends.

Snuggles the Octopus

Design by Lenka Moore

Skill Level: Intermediate

Finished Measurements:
Approx 7 inches/18 cm wide and
4 inches/10 cm tall.

Materials & Tools:
Red Heart Super Saver (100% acrylic;
7 ounces/198 g = 364 yards/333 m):
(A), 1 skein, color pumpkin #0254;
(B), small amount, color cherry red
#0319—approx 364 yards/333 m of
worsted weight yarn

- Crochet hook: 5 mm (size H-8 U.S.)
- Stitch marker
- 1 sheet each of black, white,
  and yellow craft felt
- Black sewing thread
- White sewing thread
- Sewing needle
- Yarn needle

Gauge:
Gauge is not critical for this project.

Stitches:
half double crochet (hdc)
half double crochet 2 together (hdc2tog)

Note:

Gauge is not critical for this project. Work tightly
to ensure that the stuffing does not show through
the stitches.

INSTRUCTIONS

LEGS (MAKE 8):
With A, make an adjustable ring.
Rnd 1: Work 10 hdc in ring, do not join, work in
continuous rnds—10 hdc. Place a marker in last

stitch to indicate end of round. Move marker up as each round is completed.

Rnds 2–10: Hdc in each st around.

Rnd 11: [Hdc2tog] 5 times—5 hdc.

Fasten off, leaving a 12-inch/30.5 cm tail for sewing leg to body/head

EYES (MAKE 2):

Cut out circles from white felt approx 1½ inches/ 4 cm wide. Cut out moon shapes from yellow felt, approx 1½ inches/4 cm wide, for eyelids. Cut out circles from black felt approx ½ inch/1.5 cm. With black sewing thread, sew the black circles onto the white felt circles.

BODY/HEAD:

Beginning at top of body/head, with A, make an adjustable ring.

Rnd 1: Work 8 hdc in ring, do not join, work in continuous rounds—8 hdc. Place a marker in last stitch to indicate end of round. Move marker up as each round is completed.

Rnd 2: Work 2 hdc in each st around—16 hdc.

Rnd 3: [Hdc in next st, 2 hdc in next st] 8 times—24 hdc.

Rnd 4: [Hdc in next 2 sts, 2 hdc in next st] 8 times—32 hdc.

Rnds 5–9: Hdc in each st around.

Rnd 10: [Hdc in next 2 sts, hdc2tog] 8 times— 24 hdc.

Rnd 11: [Hdc in next st, hdc2tog] 8 times—16 hdc. With B, embroider a mouth with a few straight stitches near rnd 8.

With white sewing thread, sew the white felt eyes to head, sewing over rnds 4–6. (This doesn't need to be exact.) Sew on the yellow felt eyelids.

Stuff the body/head with bunches of A, until nicely full and round.

Rnd 12: [Hdc2tog] 8 times—8 hdc.

Fasten off, leaving a long tail. Thread the tail onto yarn needle and sew opening closed.

FINISHING:

With yarn needle, sew all eight legs, one by one, to the bottom of the body/head, trying to place them evenly around the bottom. Weave in any remaining ends.

Lisa the Lion

Design by Melinda Brown

Skill Level: Intermediate

Finished Measurements:
Height 14 inches/35.5 cm, including mane and legs

Materials & Tools:
Lily Sugar 'n Cream (100% cotton; 2 ounces/ 57 g = 95 yards/86 m): (A), 2 balls, color potpourri prints #00178; (D), small amount, color black #00002—approx 190 yards/ 172 m of worsted weight yarn
Lily Sugar 'n Cream (100% cotton; 2.5 ounces/71 g = 120 yards/109 m): (B), 1 ball, color hot pink #01740; (C), 1 ball, color hot blue #01742—approx 240 yards/ 218 m of worsted weight yarn
Note: You will not need a whole ball of every color.

- Crochet hook: 4 mm (size G-6 U.S.)
- Stitch marker
- Yarn needle
- 1 small bag of stuffing

Gauge:
Gauge is not critical for this project

Stitches:
chain (ch)
single crochet (sc)
half double crochet (hdc)
half double crochet 2 together (hdc2tog)
slip stitch (sl st)
double crochet (dc)

Notes:

1. Lion is worked in six pieces: body, head, two arms, and two legs.
2. Mane is worked directly onto head. Pieces are stuffed and sewn together to form lion.
3. Gauge is not critical for this project, but work tightly so that stuffing will not show through stitches and toy is sturdy.
4. To change color, work last stitch of old color to last yarn over and draw new color through all loops on hook to complete stitch. Proceed with new color. Fasten off old color, leaving a long tail to weave in later and hide inside piece.

INSTRUCTIONS

BODY:

Beginning at bottom of body with C, ch 2.

Rnd 1: Work 6 sc in 2nd ch from hook—6 sc. Place marker in last stitch made to indicate end of round. Move marker up as each round is completed. Do not join at end of rounds, work in continuous spiral.

Rnd 2: Work 2 sc in each sc around—12 sc.

Rnd 3: [2 sc in next sc, sc in next sc] 6 times—18 sc.

Rnd 4: [2 sc in next sc, sc in next 2 sc] 6 times—24 sc.

Rnd 5: [2 sc in next sc, sc in next 3 sc] 6 times—30 sc.

Rnd 6: [2 sc in next sc, sc in next 4 sc] 6 times—36 sc.

Rnd 7: [2 sc in next sc, sc in next 5 sc] 6 times—42 sc.

Change to A.

Rnd 8: Working in front loops only, hdc in each sc around—42 hdc.

Rnds 9-13: Working in both loops, hdc in each hdc around.

Rnd 14: [Hdc2tog, hdc in next 5 hdc] 6 times—36 hdc.

Rnd 15: Hdc in each hdc around.

Rnd 16: [Hdc2tog, hdc in next 4 hdc] 6 times—30 hdc.

Rnds 17 and 18: Hdc in each hdc around.

Begin stuffing piece and continue to stuff as work progresses.

Rnd 19: [Hdc2tog, hdc in next 3 hdc] 6 times—24 hdc.

Rnds 20-22: Hdc in each hdc around.

Rnd 23: [Hdc2tog, hdc in next 2 hdc] 6 times—18 hdc.

Rnd 24: Hdc in each hdc around.

Rnd 25: [Hdc2tog, hdc in next 7 hdc] twice, sl st in next st to finish—16 hdc.

Fasten off, leaving a long tail for sewing head to body.

Head:

With A, ch 2.

Rnds 1-7: Work same as rnds 1-7 of body—42 hdc.

Rnds 8-12: Hdc in each hdc around.

Rnd 13: [Hdc2tog, hdc in next 5 hdc] 6 times—36 hdc.

Rnd 14: [Hdc2tog, hdc in next 4 hdc] 6 times—30 hdc.

Rnd 15: [Hdc2tog, hdc in next 3 hdc] 6 times—24 hdc.

Rnd 16: [Hdc2tog, hdc in next 2 hdc] 6 times—18 hdc.

Rnd 17: [Hdc2tog, hdc in next hdc] 6 times, sl st in next st to finish—12 hdc.

Fasten off and tuck tail to inside of head. Stuff head and sew to body using long tail attached to body.

MANE:

Rnd 1: Join B with sl st in head at center front of chin area, ch 1, sc in same location, work 40 sc evenly spaced around face to create base for the mane; join with sl st in first sc—40 sc.

Rnds 2 and 3: Ch 3 (counts as first dc), 2 dc in same sc as joining sl st, 3 dc in each st around; join with sl st in top of beg ch—360 dc.

Fasten off.

ARMS (MAKE 2):

With C, ch 2.

Rnds 1–3: Work same as rnds 1–3 of body—18 sc. Change to A.

Rnd 4: Working in front loops only, hdc in each sc around.

Rnds 5 and 6: Working in both loops, hdc in each hdc around.

Rnd 7: [Hdc2tog, hdc in next st] 6 times—12 hdc.

Rnds 8–13: Hdc in each hdc around.

Rnd 14: Hdc in each hdc around, sl st in next st to finish.

Fasten off, leaving a long tail for sewing arm to body.

LEGS (MAKE 2):

With B, ch 2.

Rnds 1–4: Work same as rnds 1–4 of body—24 sc. Change to A.

Rnd 5: Working in front loops only, hdc in each sc around.

Rnds 6 and 7: Working in both loops, hdc in each hdc around.

Rnd 8: [Hdc2tog, hdc in next 2 sts] 6 times—18 hdc.

Rnd 9: [Hdc2tog, hdc in next st] 6 times—12 hdc.

Rnds 10–15: Hdc in each st around.

Rnd 16: Hdc in each st around, sl st in next st to finish.

Fasten off, leaving a long tail for sewing leg to body.

Ears (make 2):

Rnd 1: Work 6 sc in 2nd ch from hook—6 sc. Place marker in last stitch made to indicate end of round. Move marker up as each round is completed. Do not join at end of rounds; work in continuous spiral.

Rnd 2: [2 sc in next sc, sc in next sc] 3 times—9 sc.

Rnd 3: Sc in each sc around.

Rnd 4: Sc in each sc around, sl st in next st to finish.

Fasten off, leaving a long tail for sewing ear to head.

FINISHING:

Using photograph as a guide for placement, sew arms and legs to body, and ears to head in front of mane.

Face:

Using photograph as a guide, thread a length of D onto yarn needle, and embroider eyes, nose, and whiskers on face.

Tail:

Cut 3 strands of yarn of colors of your choice, each about 10 inches/25.5 cm long. Hold strands together and tie to lower back of body. Braid strands together. Tie an overhand knot at end of braid to secure. Unravel the plies of the ends for a fluffy tuft at the end of the tail.

Weave in any remaining ends.

Horse Lovey

Design by Briana Olsen

Skill Level: Intermediate

Finished Measurements:
Length 16 inches/40.5 cm, measured from top of ears to lowest point

Materials & Tools:
Hobby Lobby's I Love This Yarn (100% acrylic; 7 ounces/198 g = 355 yards/321 m):

Sample 1 (purple lovey): (A), 1 ball, color periwinkle #280; (B), 1 ball, color amethyst #292; (C), 1 ball, color ivory #20; (D), small amount, color black #30—approx 1065 yards/965 m of worsted weight yarn (4) MEDIUM

Sample 2 (yellow lovey): (A), 1 ball, color sungold #156; (B), 1 ball, color buttercup #340; (C), 1 ball, color ivory #20; (D), small amount, color black #30; (E), small amount, color brown #160—approx 1065 yards/965 m of worsted weight yarn (4) MEDIUM

- **Crochet hooks:** 4 mm (size G-6 U.S.) and 5.5 mm (size I-9 U.S.)
- Tapestry Needle
- Stitch Marker
- Fiberfill

Gauge:
Gauge is not critical for this project.

Stitches:
chain (ch)
double crochet (dc)
slip stitch (sl st)
treble crochet (tr)
Front Post double treble crochet (FPdtr)*
single crochet (sc)
single crochet 2 together (sc2tog)
reverse single crochet (rsc)

*SPECIAL STITCH
Front Post double treble crochet (FPdtr):
[Yarn over] 3 times, insert hook from front to back to front again around post of indicated stitch, yarn over and draw up a loop, [yarn over and draw through 2 loops on hook] 4 times.

Notes:

1. Gauge is not critical for this project. Use a hook size recommended by the yarn manufacturer for the blanket. The blanket should measure about 18 inches/45.5 cm square. Use a hook one or two sizes smaller for the head and arms to ensure that the stuffing doesn't show through.

2. Lovey is made from four pieces: Blanket, two arms, and a head. The pieces are sewn together to complete the lovey.

3. The color is changed every round when making Blanket. Colors can be changed as frequently or infrequently as desired.

4. The color is changed while working the head to form the blaze up the center of the top of the head. To change color within a round, work last stitch of old color to last yarn over. Yarn over with new color and draw through all loops on hook to complete the stitch. Proceed with new color.

INSTRUCTIONS

BLANKET:

With A, make an adjustable ring. Work with larger hook.

Rnd 1 (RS): Ch 3 (counts as first dc here and throughout), 11 dc in ring; join with sl st in top of beg ch—12 dc. Fasten off A.

Rnd 2: With RS facing, draw up a loop of B in same st as joining, ch 3, dc in same st (increase made), (tr, FPdtr, tr) in next st, [2 dc in next 2 sts, (tr, FPdtr, tr) in next st] 3 times, 2 dc in last st; join with sl st in top of beg ch—28 sts. Fasten off B.

Rnd 3: With RS facing, draw up a loop of C in same st as joining, ch 3, dc in next dc, 2 dc in next tr, (tr, FPdtr, tr) in next FPdtr, 2 dc in next tr, [dc in next 4 dc, 2 dc in next tr, (tr, FPdtr, tr) in next FPdtr, 2 dc in next tr] 3 times, dc in last 2 dc; join with sl st in top of beg ch—44 sts. Fasten off C.

Rnd 4: With RS facing, draw up a loop of A in same st as joining, ch 3, dc in next 3 dc, 2 dc in next tr, (tr, FPdtr, tr) in next FPdtr, 2 dc in next tr, [dc in next 8 dc, 2 dc in next tr, (tr, FPdtr, tr) in next FPdtr, 2 dc in next tr] 3 times, dc in last 4 dc; join with sl st in top of beg ch—60 sts. Fasten off A.

Rnd 5: With RS facing, draw up a loop of B in same st as joining, ch 3, [dc in each dc to next tr, 2 dc in next tr, (tr, FPdtr, tr) in next FPdtr, 2 dc in next tr] 4 times, dc in each rem dc to end of rnd; join with sl st in top of beg ch—76 sts.

Rnds 6–15: Rep last rnd 10 more times and continue to change color every rnd, working next rnd with C, then [1 rnd with A, 1 rnd with B, and 1 rnd with C] 3 times.

Border:

Rnd 1: With RS facing, draw up a loop of A in same st as joining, ch 1, sc in same st as joining, work sc in each dc, 2 sc in each tr, and 3 sc in each FPdtr around; join with sl st in first sc. Fasten off A.

Rnd 2: With RS facing, draw up a loop of B in same st as joining, ch 1, rsc in each st around; join with sl st in beg ch.
Fasten off.

ARMS (MAKE 2):

With A, make an adjustable ring. Work with smaller hook.

Rnd 1: Ch 1, 6 sc in ring; join with sl st in first sc—6 sc.

Rnd 2: Ch 1, 2 sc in each sc around; join with sl st in first sc—12 sc.

Rnd 3: Ch 1, sc in BLO of each sc around; join with sl st in first sc.

Rnds 4–6: Ch 1, sc in each st around; join with sl st in first sc. Fasten off A.

Rnd 7: With RS facing, draw up a loop of B (Sample 1) or E (Sample 2) in same st as joining, ch 1, sc in each st around; do not join, work in continuous rnds for rum arm. Place marker in last stitch to indicate end of round. Move marker up as each round is completed.

Rnd 8: [Sc2tog, sc in next 4 sts] twice—10 sts.

Rnds 9–20: Sc in each st around.

Sl st in next st. Fasten off, leaving a long tail for sewing. Stuff arm and sew to rnd 1 of blanket. Sew 2nd arm directly across from first arm.

EARS (MAKE 2):

With A, make an adjustable ring. Work with smaller hook.

Rnd 1: Ch 1, 4 sc in ring; do not join, work in continuous rnds—4 sc. Place marker in last stitch to indicate end of round. Move marker up as each round is completed.

Rnd 2: [2 sc in next st, sc in next st] twice—6 sc.

Rnd 3: [2 sc in next st, sc in next 2 sts] twice—8 sc.

Rnd 4: Sc in each st around.

Rnd 5: [2 sc in next st, sc in next 3 sts] twice—10 sc.

Rnd 6: [2 sc in next st, sc in next 4 sts] twice—12 sc.

Rnds 7 and 8: Sc in each st around.

Sl st in next st. Fasten off, leaving a long tail for sewing. Flatten the ear with the yarn tail on the side. Ears can be sewn to head before or after stuffing head. To sew ears to head, use photograph as a guide to placement, pinch the bottom of the ear, and sew to head.

HEAD:

With C, make an adjustable ring. Work with smaller hook.

Nose:

Rnd 1: Ch 1, 6 sc in ring, do not join, work in continuous rnds—6 sc. Place marker in last stitch to indicate end of round. Move marker up as each round is completed.

Rnd 2: Work 2 sc in each st around—12 sc.

Rnd 3: [2 sc in next st, sc in next st] 6 times—18 sc.

Rnd 4: [2 sc in next st, sc in next 2 sts] 6 times—24 sc.

Rnds 5–8: Sc in each st around.

Begin Blaze:

Note: You will now begin to change color to form the blaze up the center of the head. When changing color, you drop the color not in use to the inside of the head and then carefully pick it up again when next needed (allowing the strands to crisscross inside the head), or you can cut and rejoin the yarn as each color change is made.

Rnd 9: With C, sc in next 3 sts; with A, 2 sc in each of the next 2 sts, sc in next 17 sts, 2 sc in each of the last 2 sts—28 sc.

Rnd 10: With C, 2 sc in next st, sc in next st, 2 sc in next st; with A, sc in last 25 sts—30 sc.

Rnd 11: With C, sc in next 5 sts; with A, 2 sc in next st, sc in next 23 sts, 2 sc in last st—32 sc.

Rnd 12: With C, sc in next 5 sts; with A, sc in last 27 sts.

Rnd 13: With C, sc in next 5 sts; with A, 2 sc in next st, sc in next 25 sts, 2 sc in last st—34 sc.

Rnd 14: With C, sc in next 5 sts; with A, sc in next 2 sts, [2 sc in next st, sc in next 7 sts] 3 times, 2 sc in next st, sc in last 2 sts—38 sc.

Rnd 15: With C, 2 sc in next st, sc in next 3 sts, 2 sc in next st; with A, sc in last 33 sts—40 sc.

Rnd 16: With C, sc in next 7 sts; with A, 2 sc in next st, sc in next 31 sts, 2 sc in last st—42 sc.

Rnd 17: With A, sc in next st; with C, sc in next 5 sts; with A, sc in last 36 sts.

Rnd 18: With A, sc in next 2 sts; with C, sc in next 3 sts; with A, sc in last 37 sts.

Rnd 19: With A, sc in next 3 sts; with C, sc in next st; with A, sc in last 38 sts. Fasten off C.

With D and using photograph as a guide, embroider eyes on each side of blaze. Stitch multiple times over top of the 3rd and 4th stitches from the sides of the C-colored blaze on rnd 14. Embroider nostrils on the sides of the nose.

Rnds 20-22: Sc in each st around.

Rnd 23: [Sc2tog, sc in next 5 sts] 6 times—36 sc.

Rnd 24: [Sc2tog, sc in next 4 sts] 6 times—30 sc.

Rnd 25: [Sc2tog, sc in next 3 sts] 6 times—24 sc. Stuff head.

Rnd 26: [Sc2tog, sc in next 2 sts] 6 times—18 sc.

Rnd 27: [Sc2tog, sc in next st] 6 times—12 sc. Add more stuffing before working next round, if needed.

Rnd 28: [Sc2tog] 6 times—6 sc.

Fasten off, leaving a long tail. Thread tail through last 6 sts and pull to close opening. Weave tail in securely. Sew ears to head if you have not already done so. Sew head over top of arms and all around rnd 1 of blanket.

Mane:
Cut 8-inch/20.5 cm lengths of B. *Insert your hook around a stitch on top of head. Fold a piece of yarn in half and place the looped end around the hook. Draw the looped end through the stitch. Draw the ends through the loop and pull tight; rep from * until mane is desired shape and thickness. The mane pictured is 3 to 4 loops thick and is from the top to the middle back of the head. Give your horse a haircut as necessary.

FINISHING:
Weave in any remaining ends.

Doily Rug

Design by Camille Jacks Morgan

Skill Level: Intermediate

Finished Measurements

Approx 36 inches/91.5 cm in diameter

Materials & Tools:

Village Yarn™ Craft Cotton Cone Yarn (100% cotton; 16 ounces/454 g = 743 yards/672 m): 3 cones, color turquoise #5050—approx 2229 yards/2016 m of worsted weight yarn ④ MEDIUM

- Crochet hook: 9 mm (size M-13 U.S.)
- Yarn needle
- Non-skid fabric spray

Gauge:

Gauge is not critical for this project.

Stitches:

chain (ch)

slip stitch (sl st)

double crochet (dc)

single crochet (sc)

half double crochet (hdc)

double crochet 2 together (dc2tog)

double crochet 3 together (dc3tog)

beginning cluster (beg-Cl)*

3 double crochet cluster (Cl)*

*SPECIAL STITCHES

Beginning cluster (beg-Cl): Ch 2, yarn over, insert hook in indicated stitch or space, yarn over and draw up a loop, yarn over and draw through 2 loops on hook (2 loops remain on hook), yarn over, insert hook in same stitch or space, yarn over and draw up a loop, yarn over and draw through 2 loops on hook, yarn over and draw through all 3 loops on hook.

3 double crochet cluster (Cl): Yarn over, insert hook in indicated stitch or space, yarn over and draw up a loop, yarn over and draw through 2 loops on hook (2 loops remain on hook), *yarn over, insert hook in same stitch or space, yarn over and draw up a loop, yarn over and draw through 2 loops on hook; rep from * once more, yarn over and draw through all 4 loops on hook.

Notes:

1. Rug is worked with 3 strands of yarn held together throughout.
2. Rug is worked in joined rounds, beginning at center.

INSTRUCTIONS

Holding 3 strands of yarn together, work as follows:

Ch 5; join with a sl st in first ch to form a ring.

Rnd 1: Ch 3 (counts as first dc here and throughout), work 17 dc in ring; join with sl st in top of beg ch-3—18 dc.

Rnd 2: Ch 1, sc in same st as joining, 2 sc in next dc, *sc in next dc, 2 sc in next dc; rep from * around; join with sl st in beg ch-1—27 sc.

Rnd 3: Ch 2, dc2tog, *ch 4, dc3tog; rep from *around, ch 4; join with sl st in top of first dc2tog—9 "petals" and 9 ch-4 sps.

Rnd 4: Beg-Cl in same st as joining, ch 2, (Cl, ch 2, Cl, ch 2, Cl) in next ch-4 sp, *ch 2, Cl in next dc3tog, ch 2, (Cl, ch 2, Cl, ch 2, Cl) in next ch-4 sp; rep from * around; join with hdc in top of beg-Cl—36 clusters and 36 ch-2 sps. Note: The joining hdc counts as a ch-2 sp. When instructed to work in this ch-2 sp, work around the post of the hdc.

Rnds 5 and 6: Beg-Cl in first ch-2 sp (formed by the joining hdc), *ch 2, Cl in next ch-2 sp; rep from * around; join with hdc in top of beg-Cl.

Rnd 7: Beg-Cl in first ch-2 sp, *ch 3, Cl in next ch-2 sp; rep from * around, ch 3; join with sl st in top of beg-Cl—36 clusters and 36 ch-3 sps.

Rnd 8: (Sl st, 3 sc) in first ch-3 sp, 3 sc in each ch-3 sp around; join with sl st in first sc—108 sc.

Rnd 9: Ch 1, sc in same st as joining, sc in each sc around; join with sl st in first sc.

Rnd 10: Beg-Cl in same st as joining, *ch 3, sk next 2 sc, Cl in next sc; rep from * around to last 2 sc, ch 3, sk last 2 sc; join with sl st in top of beg-Cl—36 clusters and 36 ch-3 sps.

Rnd 11: (Sl st, ch 3, 4 dc) in first ch-3 sp, ch 2, sc in next ch-3 sp, *ch 2, 5 dc in next ch-3 sp, ch 2, sc in next ch-3 sp; rep from * around, ch 2; join with sl st in top of beg ch-3—90 dc, 18 sc, and 36 ch-2 sps.

Rnd 12: Ch 4 (counts as dc, ch 1), dc in next dc, [ch 1, dc in next dc] 3 times, *ch 1, sk next 2 ch-2 sps, dc in next dc, [ch 1, dc in next dc] 4 times; rep from * around to last 2 ch-3 sps, ch 1, sk last 2 ch-3 sps; join with sl st in 3rd ch of beg ch-4—90 dc and 90 ch-1 sps.

Rnd 13: Sl st in first ch-1 sp, [ch 3, sc in next ch-1 sp] 3 times, ch 1, 2 dc in next ch-1 sp, *ch 1, sc in next ch-1 sp, [ch 3, sc in next ch-1 sp] 3 times, ch 1, 2 dc in next ch-1 sp; rep from * around, ch 1; join with sl st in first sl st.

Rnd 14: Sl st to 2nd ch of first ch-3, [ch 3, sc in next ch-3 sp] twice, ch 1, (2 dc, ch 1, 2 dc) in sp between next 2 dc sts, *ch 1, sc in next ch-3 sp, [ch 3, sc in next ch-3 sp] twice, ch 1, (2 dc, ch 1, 2 dc) in sp between next 2 dc sts; rep from * around, ch 1; join with sl st in first sl st.

Rnd 15: Sl st to 2nd ch of first ch-3, ch 3, sc in next ch-3 sp, ch 3, sk next ch-1 sp, (2 dc, ch 2, 2 dc) in next ch-1 sp (between 2-dc groups), *ch 3, sk next ch-1 sp, sc in next ch-3 sp, ch 3, sc in next ch-3 sp, ch 3, sk next ch-1 sp, sk next ch-1 sp, (2 dc, ch 2, 2 dc) in next ch-1 sp; rep from * around, ch 3; join with sl st in first sl st.

Rnd 16: Sl st to 2nd ch of first ch-3, *(2 hdc, ch 1, 2 hdc) in next ch-3 sp, (2 dc, ch 2, 2 dc) in next ch-2 sp, (2 hdc, ch 1, 2 hdc) in next ch-3 sp **, sc in next ch-3 sp; rep from * around, ending last rep at **; join with sl st in first sl st.
Fasten off.

FINISHING:
Weave in ends. Apply non-skid spray to back side of rug, per manufacturer's instructions.

Granny Squares Pillow

Design by Annamarie Haakblog

Skill Level: Intermediate

Finished Measurement:
12 inches/30.5 cm square

Materials & Tools:
Schachenmayr Catania (100% cotton;
1.75 ounces/50 g = 137 yards/125 m)
and Phildar Coton 3 (100% cotton; 1.75
ounces/50 g = 132 yards/121 m): multiple
balls or partial balls of colors of your
choice—approx 540 yards/494 m of
double-knit weight yarn

- Crochet hook: 2.75 mm (size C-2 U.S.)
- Sewing needle
- Pillow form, 12 inches/30.5 cm square

Gauge:
One granny square on front of pillow
measures about 3½ inches/9 cm square.
Always take time to check your gauge.

Stitches:
chain (ch)
single crochet (sc)
slip stitch (sl st)
double crochet (dc)

Notes:

1. Front is made from nine smaller granny squares. Back is made from one large granny square.
2. The granny squares are worked in joined rounds, using a different color for each round.
3. Use any colors you wish. If you would like your pillow to look similar to the pillow shown, do not use the same color at the same position in any two granny squares.
4. When instructed to "join with sc" work as follows: Place a slip knot of the new color on your hook, insert the hook in the indicated

location, yarn over and draw up a loop (2 loops on hook), yarn over and draw through both loops on hook.

INSTRUCTIONS

FRONT GRANNY SQUARES (MAKE 9)

With color of your choice, ch 6; join with sl st in first ch to form a ring.

Rnd 1 (RS): Ch 3 (counts as first dc), work 11 more dc in ring; join with sl st in top of beg ch—12 dc. Fasten off.

Rnd 2: With RS facing, join next color with sc in any sp between dc of previous rnd, ch 2 (counts as first dc here and throughout), dc in same sp, work 2 dc in each rem sp between dc around; join with sl st in top of beg ch—24 dc (twelve 2-dc groups). Fasten off.

Rnd 3: With RS facing, join next color with sc in any sp between 2-dc groups, ch 2, 2 dc in same sp between groups, 3 dc in each rem sp between 2-dc groups around; join with sl st in top of beg ch—36 dc (twelve 3-dc groups). Fasten off.

Rnd 4: With RS facing, join next color with sc in any sp between 3-dc groups, ch 2, 3 dc in same sp between groups, 4 dc in each rem sp between 3-dc groups around; join with sl st in top of beg ch—48 dc (twelve 4-dc groups). Fasten off.

Rnd 5: With RS facing, join next color with sl st in any sp between 4-dc groups, ch 3, 2 dc in same sp between groups, ch 1, (3 dc, ch 3, 3 dc) in next sp between 4-dc groups (corner made) *[ch 1, 3 dc in next sp between 4-dc groups] twice, ch 1, (3 dc, ch 3, 3 dc) in next sp between 4-dc groups; rep from * 2 more times, ch 1, 3 dc in last sp

between 4-dc groups; join with sl st in top of beg ch—4 corners and two 3-dc groups across each side between corners. Do NOT fasten off.

Rnd 6: Continuing with same color, ch 1, *sc in each dc and ch-1 sp to next corner ch-3 sp, (sc, ch 1, sc) in corner ch-3 sp; rep from * 3 more times, sc in each rem dc and ch-1 sp to end of rnd; join with sl st in first sc—68 sc and 4 corner ch-1 sps. Fasten off.

Assembly:

Arrange granny squares into three rows of three squares each. Working from WS, hold two neighbouring squares with RS together and stitches matching across edge to be joined. Working through both thicknesses, join color of your choice with sc in first st at beg of edge to be joined, sc across edge to join square. Rep this process until all squares have been joined to a large square consisting of three rows of three squares each.

Outer Edging:

Rnd 1: With RS facing, join color of your choice in any sc of outer edge, sc in each sc all the way around, skipping the ch-2 sps at all corners; join with sl st in first sc—204 sc (51 sc across each side of large square, 17 sc across outer edge of each granny square). Fasten off.

Rnd 2: With RS facing, join color of your choice with sl st in 2nd sc of any corner, ch 3, 2 dc in same corner sc, **sk next 2 sc, *3 dc in next sc, sk next 2 sc; rep from * to 2 sc of next corner, 3 dc in first sc of corner ***, ch 3, 3 dc in next sc of corner; rep from ** around ending last rep at ***; join with sl st in top of beg ch—72 groups (eighteen 3-dc groups across each side). Fasten off.

BACK:

With color of your choice, ch 4; join with sl st in first ch to form ring.

Rnd 1 (RS): Ch 3 (counts as first dc), 2 dc in ring, [ch 2, 3 dc in ring] 3 times, ch 2; join with sl st in top of beg ch—12 dc (four 3-dc groups). Fasten off.

Rnd 2: With RS facing, join next color with sl st in any corner ch-2 sp, ch 4 (counts as dc, ch 1), *(3 dc, ch 2, 3 dc) in next ch-2 sp (corner made), ch 1; rep from * 2 more times, (3 dc, ch 2, 2 dc) in same ch-2 sp as joining (last corner completed); join with sl st in 3rd ch of beg ch—24 dc (eight 3-dc groups). Fasten off.

Rnd 3: With RS facing, join next color with sl st in any corner ch-2 sp, ch 5 (counts as dc, ch 2 here and throughout), 3 dc in same ch-2 sp, ch 1, 3 dc in next ch-1 sp, *ch 1, (3 dc, ch 2, 3 dc) in next ch-2 sp, ch 1, 3 dc in next ch-1 sp; rep from * 2 more times, ch 1, 2 dc in same ch-2 sp as joining; join with sl st in 3rd ch of beg ch—36 dc (twelve 3-dc groups). Fasten off.

Rnd 4: With RS facing, join next color with sl st in any corner ch-2 sp, ch 5, 3 dc in same ch-2 sp, [ch 1, 3 dc in next ch-1 sp] twice, *ch 1, (3 dc, ch 2, 3 dc) in next ch-2 sp, [ch 1, 3 dc in next ch-1 sp] twice; rep from * 2 more times, ch 1, 2 dc in same ch-2 sp as joining; join with sl st in 3rd ch of beg ch—48 dc (sixteen 3-dc groups). Fasten off.

Rnd 5: With RS facing, join next color with sl st in any corner ch-2 sp, ch 5, 3 dc in same ch-2 sp, [ch 1, 3 dc in next ch-1 sp] to next corner ch-2 sp, *ch 1, (3 dc, ch 2, 3 dc) in next ch-2 sp, [ch 1, 3 dc in next ch-1 sp] to next corner ch-2 sp; rep from * 2 more times, ch 1, 2 dc in same ch-2 sp as joining; join

with sl st in 3rd ch of beg ch—60 dc (twenty 3-dc groups). Fasten off.

Rnds 6–17: Rep last rnd 12 more times—204 dc (sixty-eight 3-dc groups)

Rnd 18: Using same color as used in last rnd of front, rep rnd 5 once more—216 dc (seventy-two 3-dc groups, 18 groups across each edge). Fasten off.

FINISHING

Weave in ends.

Assembly and Optional Edging:

Using same color as last round of front and back, sew the front and back together or make an edging by working 1 sc in each sc around, joining round with sl st in first sc. Insert pillow form before seaming 4th edge.

Dream Mobile

Design by Emma Lamb

Skill Level: Easy
Finished Measurements:
Motifs: 1¼–1¾ inches/3–4.5 cm
Mobile: approx 22 inches/56 cm long and
8 inches/20.5 cm wide.

Materials & Tools:
DMC Natura Just Cotton (100% cotton;
1.75 ounces/50 g = 170 yards/155 m): (A),
1 ball, color Ibiza #01; (B), 1 ball, color rose
layette #06; (C), 1 ball, color tournesol
#16; (D), 1 ball, color coral #18; (E), 1 ball,
color aquamarina #25; (F), 1 ball, color
canelle #37; (G), 1 ball, color safron #47;
(H), 1 ball, color chartreuse #48—approx
1360 yards/1240 m of sock weight yarn 🧶
SUPER FINE
Note: You will not need a whole ball of
each color.

- Crochet hook: 3.25 mm (size D-3 U.S.) or
  size to obtain gauge
- Wooden embroidery hoop, 8 inches/20.5 cm
  diameter (inner solid hoop part only)
- Yarn needle
- Pins

Gauge:
Flower motifs should measure approx 1¾
inches/4.5 cm in diameter. Gauge is not
critical for this project.

Stitches:
chain (ch)
treble crochet (tr)
slip stitch (sl st)
single crochet (sc)
half double crochet (hdc)
double crochet (dc)
2 treble crochet cluster (CL)*
picot*

*SPECIAL STITCHES
2 treble crochet cluster (CL) [Yarn over]
twice, insert hook in indicated stitch and
draw up a loop, [yarn over and draw
through 2 loops on hook] twice (2 loops
on hook), [yarn over] twice, insert hook
in same stitch and draw up a loop, [yarn
over and draw through 2 loops on hook]
twice, yarn over and draw through all 3
loops on hook.

Picot: Ch 3, sl st in top of last sc made.

Notes:

1. Mobile is made from 35 motifs that are strung into 7 trails of 5 motifs each. The inner ring of the embroidery hoop is covered with a strip of crochet, and the trails are attached to the lower edge of the hoop. Two hanging cords and a center hanging loop are attached to the upper edge of the hoop.
2. Accurate gauge is not essential for this project; however, it is better to aim to match the specified gauge for a neater finished product.

INSTRUCTIONS

FLOWER MOTIF (MAKE 8—1 EACH WITH A, B, C, D, E, F, G, AND H):

Make an adjustable ring.

Rnd 1: Ch 4, tr in ring (beg ch and first tr combine to count as first Cl), [ch 4, Cl in ring] 5 times, ch 4, pull on beg tail to tighten ring; join with sl st in top of first Cl—6 Cl and 6 ch-4 sps.

Rnd 2: Ch 1, (sc, hdc, 3 dc, hdc, sc) in each ch-4 sp around; join with sl st in first sc—6 petals.
Fasten off and weave in ends.

STAR MOTIF (MAKE 8—1 EACH WITH A, B, C, D, E, F, G, AND H):

Ch 6; join with sl st in first ch to form a ring.

Rnd 1: Ch 2 (counts as first sc), 14 sc in ring; join with sl st in beg ch-2—15 sts.

Rnd 2: Ch 6 (counts as hdc, ch 4), sk same st as joining, sk next sc, hdc in next st, ch 4, *sk next 2 sts, hdc in next st, ch 4; rep from * around; join with sl st in 2nd ch of beg ch-6—5 sts and 5 ch-4 sps.

Rnd 3: Ch 1, (sc, hdc, dc, ch 2, dc, hdc, sc) in each ch-4 sp around, join with sl st in first sc—5 points. Fasten off and weave in ends. To make star points more "pointy," insert hook into ch-2 space at tip of point and pull into shape.

CIRCLE MOTIF (MAKE 8—1 EACH WITH A, B, C, D, E, F, G, AND H):

Make an adjustable ring.

Rnd 1: Ch 1, 6 sc in ring, pull on beg tail to tighten ring; join with sl st in first sc—6 sts.

Rnd 2: Ch 7 (counts as dc, ch 4), *dc in next st, ch 4; rep from * around; join with sl st in 3rd ch of beg ch-7—6 sts and 6 ch-4 sps.

Rnd 3: Ch 1, 5 sc in each ch-4 sp around, join with sl st in first sc—30 sts.

Rnd 4: Ch 1, begin in same st as joining, *sc in next 4 sts, 2 sc into next st; rep from * around; join with sl st in first sc—36 sts.
Fasten off and weave in ends.

MINI HEXAGON MOTIF (MAKE 16—2 EACH WITH A, B, C, D, E, F, G, AND H):

Ch 5; join with sl st in first ch to form a ring.

Rnd 1: Ch 3 (counts as first dc), 11 dc in ring; join with sl st in top of beg ch-3—12 sts.

Rnd 2: Ch 1, beg in same st as joining, *sc in next st, picot, sc in next st; rep from * around; join with sl st in first sc—12 sc and 6 picots.
Fasten off and weave in loose ends.

MOBILE HOOP HEADER COVER:

With A, ch 9.

Foundation row: Sc in 2nd ch from hook and in each ch across—8 sc.

Rows 2–15: Ch 1, turn, sc in each sc across.

Note: Strip should measure approx 22½ inches/ 57 cm, a little shorter than the circumference of the hoop, to ensure that the header cover is neat and not baggy.

Fasten off and weave in ends. Making sure that header cover crochet strip is not twisted, neatly sew together the two short ends to form a ring. Fold the ring in half lengthwise and sandwich the wooden hoop inside; it may need to be stretched a little to do this.

Joining rnd: With the hoop inside the crochet strip and working through both thicknesses (both long side edges), join A with sc anywhere in edges, sc in each st around; join with sl st in first sc. Fasten off. The joining round marks the top of the mobile, where the hanging cords will be attached.

HANGING CORDS AND LOOP (MAKE 2):

Leaving a long beg tail for sewing to header hoop, with A, ch 60; sl st in 15th ch from hook to form a center ring, ch 45. Fasten off, leaving a long tail for sewing to header hoop.

Center ring: Holding 2 center rings together, join A with sc through both rings, work 24 more sc through both rings; join with sl st in first sc. Fasten off.

Mark 4 evenly spaced points with pins on your header hoop. Then using the yarn needle, securely sew your hanging cords to your header.

FINISHING:

Flower Trails:

Arrange the motifs into 7 groups of 5 motifs each, with 1 flower, 1 star, 1 circle, and 2 mini hexagons in each group arranged in the following order: flower, hexagon, star, hexagon, and circle. I like to arrange the colors so that there is no more than 1 motif of each color in each group.

To string the motifs together, join A in any edge st of circle motif, ch 25, sl st in edge of hexagon motif, ch 25, sl st in any point of star motif, ch 25, sl st in edge of 2nd hexagon motif, ch 25, sl st in tip of any petal flower motif, ch 15.

Fasten off. Repeat for seven flower trails.

Mark 7 evenly spaced points with pins on the underside of the header hoop. Then using the yarn needle, securely sew your flower trails to the header.

Weave in any remaining ends.

Stars & Blossom Garland

Design by Emma Lamb

Skill Level: Easy
Finished Measurements:
Motifs: 1¼–1¾ inches/3–4.5 cm
Garland: approx 43 inches/109 cm.

Materials and Tools:
Girl's Garland:
Anchor Perle Cotton #5 (100% cotton; 0.17 ounce/5 g = 23 yards/21 m): 1 skein each of: (A), color off white #2; (B), color bubblegum pink #23; (C), color shocking pink #28; (D), color pale yellow #295; (E), sunny yellow #302; (F), color tangerine orange #330; (G), color cream #926—approx 161 yards/147 m of lace weight yarn.
Note: You will not need a whole skein of every color.

Boy's Garland:
Anchor Perle Cotton #5 (100% cotton; 0.17 ounce/5 g = 23 yards/21 m): 1 skein each of: (A), color off white #2; (B), color ultramarine #134; (C), color sky blue #167; (D), color bright turquoise #187; (E), color neon lime #278; (F), color sunny yellow #302; (G), color cream #926—approx 161 yards/147 m of lace weight yarn.
Note: You will not need a whole ball of every color.

- Crochet hooks: 3.25 mm (size D-3 U.S.) and 1.5 mm (size 7 US) or size to obtain gauge Yarn needle
- Sewing needle

Gauge:
Circle motifs should measure approximately 1½ inches/4 cm in diameter.
Gauge is not critical for this project.

Stitches:
chain (ch)
slip stitch (sl ss)
single crochet (sc)
half double crochet (hdc)
double crochet (dc)
2 double crochet clusters (Cl)*
picot*

*SPECIAL STITCHES
2 double crochet clusters (Cl): Yarn over, insert hook in indicated stitch and draw up a loop, yarn over and draw through 2 loops on hook (2 loops on hook), yarn over, insert hook in same stitch and draw up a loop, yarn over and draw through 2 loops on hook, yarn over and draw through all 3 loops on hook.

Picot: Ch 3, sc in 3rd ch from hook.

Notes:

1. All motifs are worked with two strands of thread held together, with one strand changed to a new color at the beginning of the last round. Change color by knotting two threads together and ensuring that your knot is as close to your work as possible; this will make it easier to hide when you come to weave in your loose ends.
2. Each garland is made from 13 motifs. Make motifs using color combinations indicated below, for Girl's and Boy's Garland.
3. Accurate gauge is not essential for this project; however, it is better to aim to match the specified gauge for a neater finished product.

Girl's Garland
(make 13 motifs of the following types and color combinations)
- motif 1 (make 3): Flower, with colors C, F, G
- motif 2 (make 2): Star, D, G, B
- motif 3 (make 2): Circle, F, C, E
- motif 4 (make 2): Flower, B, E, G
- motif 5 (make 2): Star, B, E, C
- motif 6 (make 2): Circle, D, F, E

Boy's Garland
(make 13 motifs of the following types and color combinations)
- motif 1 (make 3): Star, with colors C, D, B
- motif 2 (make 2): Flower, G, C, F
- motif 3 (make 2): Circle, C, B, E
- motif 4 (make 2): Star, G, E, F
- motif 5 (make 2): Flower, C, F, D
- motif 6 (make 2): Circle, E, D, F

INSTRUCTIONS

CIRCLE MOTIF:
With larger hook and one strand each of first 2 colors held together, Ch 5; join with a sl st in first ch to form a ring.
Rnd 1: Ch 3 (counts as first dc here and throughout), work 11 dc in ring, join with sl st in top of beg ch-3—12 sts.
Change 2nd color to 3rd color. Hold one strand each of first and 3rd colors together.

Rnd 2: Ch 3, dc in same st as joining, 2 dc in each st around; join with sl st in top of beg ch-3—24 sts. Fasten off and weave in ends.

FLOWER MOTIF:

With larger hook and one strand each of first 2 colors held together, Ch 5; join with a sl st in first ch to form a ring.

Rnd 1: Ch 1, work 7 sc in ring; join with a sl st in first sc—7 sts.

Rnd 2: Ch 6 (counts as dc, ch 3), *dc in next st, ch 3; rep from * around; join with sl st in 3rd ch of beg ch-6—7 dc and 7 ch-3 sps.

Change 2nd color to 3rd color. Hold one strand each of first and 3rd colors together.

Rnd 3: Ch 1, (sc, hdc, 2 dc, hdc, sc) in each ch-3 sp around; join with sl st in first sc—7 petals. Fasten off and weave in ends.

STAR MOTIF:

With larger hook and one strand each of first 2 colors held together, Ch 5; join with a sl st in first ch to form a ring.

Rnd 1: Ch 2, dc in ring (beg ch and first dc combine to count as first Cl), [Cl in ring, ch 3] 4 times; join with sl st in top of first Cl—5 Cl and 5 ch-3 sps.

Change 2nd color to 3rd color. Hold one strand each of first and 3rd colors together.

Rnd 2: Ch 1, (sc, hdc, dc, picot, dc, hdc, sc) in each ch-3 sp around; join with sl st in first sc— 5 points.

Fasten off and weave in ends.

FINISHING:

With smaller hook and A, arrange motifs in order as indicated in color combination list(s) (above): placing one motif 1 first, one motif 2, one motif 3, one motif 4, one motif 5, one motif 6, and repeating until all 13 motifs have been arranged in order.

String Motifs: Ch 30; join with sl st in first ch to form a ring (for hanging loop), *ch 35, dc in edge of next motif; rep from * 10 more times, ch 65, sl st in 30th ch from hook (for 2nd hanging loop). Fasten off and weave in ends.

Big Granny Square Blanket

Design by Ilaria Chiaratti

Skill Level: Beginner
Finished Measurements:
31 inches/79 cm square

Materials & Tools:
Annell Rapido (100% acrylic; 1.75
ounces/50 g = 145 yards/133 m):
(A), 2 balls, color light pink #3233;
(B), 2 balls, color pink #3277; (C), 2 balls,
color orange #3221; (D), 2 balls, color light
gray #3356; (E), 2 balls, color turquoise
#3222; (F), 2 balls, color blue peacock
#3262; (G), 1 ball, color white #3260—
approx 1885 yards/1710 m double-knit
weight yarn 🧶**3**
LIGHT

• **Crochet hook:** 4 mm (size G-6 U.S.)

Gauge: Gauge is not critical for this
project.

Stitches:
chain (ch)
double crochet (dc)
slip stitch (sl st)

Notes:

1. Blanket is made from four large granny
    squares.
2. The granny squares are joined together using
    a "join as you go" technique while working the
    last round of the square.

INSTRUCTIONS

FIRST GRANNY SQUARE:
With A, ch 4; join with sl st in first ch to form a ring.
Rnd 1 (RS): Ch 3 (counts as first dc here and
throughout), 2 dc in ring, [ch 3, 3 dc in ring] 3
times, ch 3; join with sl st in top of beg ch-3—12 dc
and 4 ch-3 sps.
Rnd 2: Sl st in next 2 dc, (sl st, ch 3, 2 dc, ch 3, 3
dc) in first ch-3 sp (first corner made), *ch 1, (3
dc, ch 3, 3 dc) in next ch-3 sp (corner made); rep
from * 2 more times, ch 1; join with sl st in top of
beg ch-3—4 corners.
Rnd 3: Sl st in next 2 dc, (sl st, ch 3, 2 dc, ch 3, 3
dc) in first ch-3 sp (corner made), *ch 1, 3 dc in
next ch-1 sp, ch 1, (3 dc, ch 3, 3 dc) in next ch-3 sp;
rep from * 2 more times, ch 1, 3 dc in last ch-1 sp,
ch 1; join with sl st in top of beg ch-3—one 3-dc
group on each side between corners. Fasten off.
Rnd 4 (RS): With RS facing, draw up a loop of
B in any corner ch-3 sp, ch 3, (2 dc, ch 3, 3 dc) in
same ch-3 sp, *(ch 1, 3 dc in next ch-1 sp) to next
corner ch-3 sp, ch 1, (3 dc, ch 3, 3 dc) in corner
ch-3 sp; rep from * 2 more times, (ch 1, 3 dc in
next ch-1 sp) to end of rnd, ch 1; join with sl st in
top of beg ch-3—two 3-dc groups on each side
between corners.

Rnds 5 and 6: Sl st in next 2 dc, (sl st, ch 3, 2 dc, ch 3, 3 dc) in first ch-3 sp (corner made), *(ch 1, 3 dc in next ch-1 sp) to next corner ch-3 sp, ch 1, (3 dc, ch 3, 3 dc) in corner ch-3 sp; rep from * 2 more times, (ch 1, 3 dc in last ch-1 sp) to end of rnd, ch 1; join with sl st in top of beg ch-3—four 3-dc groups on each side between corners. Fasten off at the end of rnd 6.

Rnds 7–9: With C, rep rnds 4–6. Fasten off at the end of rnd 9—seven 3-dc groups on each side between corners.

Rnds 10–12: With D, rep rnds 4–6. Fasten off at the end of rnd 12—ten 3-dc groups on each side between corners.

Rnds 13–15: With E, rep rnds 4–6. Fasten off at the end of rnd 15—thirteen 3-dc groups on each side between corners.

Rnds 16–18: With F, rep rnds 4–6. Fasten off at the end of rnd 18—sixteen 3-dc groups on each side between corners.

Rnd 19: With G, rep rnd 4—seventeen 3-dc groups on each side between corners. Fasten off.

SECOND GRANNY SQUARE:

Work same as first granny square through rnd 18, working rnds 1–3 with B, rnds 4–6 with C, rnds 7–9 with E, rnds 10–12 with F, rnds 13–15 with D, and rnds 16–18 with A.

Notes: 1. The final round is now worked and one edge of this granny square is joined to one edge of the first granny square as the final round is worked. 2. When working the joining edge, hold the granny squares with wrong sides together and stitches matching. Hold the squares with the second square facing you and the first square behind.

Rnd 19 (joining rnd): With RS facing, draw up a loop of G in any corner ch-3 sp, ch 3, (2 dc, ch 3, 3 dc) in same ch-3 sp, (ch 1, 3 dc in next ch-1 sp) to next corner ch-3 sp. Joining edge to first granny square: 3 dc in corner ch-3 sp, sl st in corresponding corner ch-3 sp of first granny square, 3 dc in same corner ch-3 sp of current square, (sl st in next ch-1 sp of first granny square, 3 dc in next ch-1 sp of current square) to next corner ch-3 sp, sl st in next ch-1 sp of first granny square, 3 dc in next corner ch-3 sp, sl st in corresponding corner ch-3 sp of first granny square, 3 dc in same corner ch-3 sp of current square.
Complete joining rnd: (ch 1, 3 dc in next ch-1 sp) to next corner ch-3 sp, ch 1, (3 dc, ch 3, 3 dc) in next corner ch-3 sp, (ch 1, 3 dc in next ch-1 sp) to end of rnd, ch 1, join with sl st in top of beg ch-3.

THIRD GRANNY SQUARE:

Work same as first granny square through rnd 18, working rnds 1–3 with F, rnds 4–6 with D, rnds 7–9 with B, rnds 10–12 with A, rnds 13–15 with C, and rnds 16–18 with E.
Rnd 19 (joining rnd): Work same as rnd 19 of second granny square, joining to second granny square as you go.

FOURTH GRANNY SQUARE:

Work same as first granny square through rnd 18, working rnds 1–3 with E, rnds 4–6 with B, rnds 7–9 with A, rnds 10–12 with C, rnds 13–15 with F, and rnds 16–18 with D.

Rnd 19 (joining rnd): Work same as rnd 19 of second granny square, joining one edge to third granny square and one edge to first granny square as you go.

FINISHING:

Border:

With RS facing, draw up a loop of G in any corner ch-3 sp, ch 3, (2 dc, ch 3, 3 dc) in same corner ch-3 sp, *dc in each dc and ch-sp (including the joined corner ch-3 sps) to next corner ch-3 sp, (3 dc, ch 3, 3 dc) in corner ch-3 sp; rep from * 2 more times, dc in each dc and ch-sp to end of rnd; join with sl st in top of beg ch-3. Fasten off. Weave in ends.

Wavy Stripes Baby Blanket

Design by Maaike van Koert

Skill Level: Easy
Finished Measurements:
25 x 20 inches/64 x 51 cm

Materials & Tools:
Schachenmayr Catania (100% mercerized cotton; 1.75 ounces/50 g = 133 yards/125 m): (A), 2 balls, color white #106; (B), 1 ball, color canary #208; (C), 1 ball, color light pink #246; (D), 1 ball, color orange #189; (E), 1 ball, color turquoise #146; (F), 1 ball, color navy #124; (G), 1 ball, color pool #165; (H), 1 ball, color sea green #241; (I), 1 ball, color jade #253—approx 1330 yards/1250 m sport weight yarn

- Crochet hook: 3 mm (size D U.S.) or size to obtain gauge
- Yarn needle

Gauge:
22 sts = 4 inches/10 cm and 12 rows = 3½ inches/9 cm
Always take time to check your gauge.

Stitches:
chain (ch)
double crochet (dc)
treble crochet (tr)
single crochet (sc)
slip stitch (sl st)

Note:

To change color, work last stitch of old color to last yarn over. Yarn over with new color and draw through all loops on hook to complete stitch. Proceed with new color. Fasten off old color.

INSTRUCTIONS

With I, ch 101.

Row 1: Dc in 3rd ch from hook (beg ch counts as first dc), dc in each ch across—100 dc.

Rows 2 and 3: Ch 2 (counts as first dc here and throughout), turn, dc in each dc across (working last dc in top of beg ch-2); change to F in last st of row 3.

Row 4: With F, ch 2, turn, dc in next dc, *sk next st, 2 dc in next st; rep from * across; change to I in last st—fifty 2-dc groups.

Row 5: With I, ch 2, turn, dc in next dc, *dc in next sp between 2-dc groups, dc in next dc; rep from * across—100 dc.

Rows 6 and 7: Ch 2, turn, dc in each dc across; change to D in last st of row 7.

Row 8: With D, ch 2, turn, dc in each dc across.

Row 9: Ch 2, turn, dc in next dc, *tr in next 2 dc, dc in next 2 dc, sc in next 2 dc, dc in next 2 dc; rep from * to last 2 dc, tr in last 2 dc; change to A in last st—11 full waves and one half wave at each end of row.

Row 10: With A, ch 1, turn, sc in each st across; change to C in last st.

Row 11: With C, ch 2, turn, dc in next st, *sc in next 2 sts, dc in next 2 sts, tr in next 2 sts, dc in next 2 sts; rep from * to last 2 sts, sc in last 2 sts—12 waves.

Row 12: Ch 1, turn, dc in each st across; change to H in last st.

Rows 13–15: With H, ch 2, turn, dc in each st across; change to E in last st of row 15.

Row 16: With E, rep row 4; change to H in last st.

Rows 17–19: With H, rep rows 5–7; change to C in last st of row 19.

Rows 20 and 21: With C, rep rows 8 and 9; change to A in last st of row 21.

Row 22: Rep row 10; change to B in last st.

Rows 23 and 24: With B, rep rows 11 and 12; change to G in last st of row 24.

Rows 25–27: With G, rep rows 13–15; change to F in last st of row 27.

Row 28: With F, rep row 4; change to G in last st.

Rows 29–31: With G rep rows 5–7; change to D in last st of row 31.

Rows 32 and 33: With D, rep rows 8 and 9; change to A in last st of row 33.

Row 34: Rep row 10; change to C in last st.

Rows 35 and 36: With C, rep rows 11 and 12; change to E in last st of row 36.

Rows 37–39: With E, rep rows 13–15; change to A in last st of row 39.

Row 40: With A, rep row 4; change to E in last st.

Rows 41–43: With E rep rows 5–7; change to C in last st of row 43.

Rows 44 and 45: With C, rep rows 8 and 9; change to A in last st of row 45.

Row 46: Rep row 10; change to D in last st.

Rows 47 and 48: With D, rep rows 11 and 12; change to I in last st of row 48.

Rows 49–51: With I, rep rows 13–15; change to F in last st of row 51.

Row 52: With F, rep row 4; change to I in last st.

Rows 53–55: With I, rep rows 5–7; change to B in last st of row 55.

Rows 56 and 57: With B, rep rows 8 and 9; change to A in last st of row 57.

Row 58: Rep row 10; change to C in last st.

Rows 59 and 60: With C, rep rows 11 and 12; change to H in last st of row 60.

Rows 61–63: With H, rep rows 13–15; change to E in last st of row 63.

Row 64: With E, rep row 4; change to H in last st.

Rows 65–67: With H rep rows 5–7; change to C in last st of row 67.

Rows 68 and 69: With C, rep rows 8 and 9; change to A in last st of row 69.

Row 70: With A, rep row 10; change to D in last st.

Rows 71 and 72: With D, rep rows 11 and 12; change to G in last st of row 72.

Rows 73–75: With G, rep rows 13–15; change to F in last st of row 75.

Row 76: With F, rep row 4; change to G in last st.

Rows 77–79: With G, rep rows 5–7. Fasten off.

EDGING:

Rnd 1: With RS facing, draw up a loop of A anywhere in one long edge of blanket, ch 2, dc evenly spaced around by working 2 dc in the end of each dc row, and dc in the end of each sc row across long edges, dc in each st across short edges, and at each corner work 2 dc in row end or st before corner, 3 dc in corner, and 2 dc in row end or st following corner; join with sl st in top of beg ch-2.

Rnd 2: Ch 2, dc in each st around, working 3-dc corners as follows: 2 dc in first dc of 3-dc corner, 3 dc in next dc, 2 dc in last dc of 3-dc corner; join with sl st in top of beg ch-2. Fasten off.

FINISHING:

Weave in ends.

Organic Stripes Blanket

Design by Sierra Gallagher

Skill Level: Beginner
Finished Measurements:
22 inches/56 cm square

Materials & Tools:
Blue Sky Alpacas Worsted Cotton (100% certified organic cotton; 3.5 ounces/100 g = 150 yards/137 m): (A), 2 skeins, color bone #80; (B), 2 skeins, color sleet #635; (C), 2 skeins, color lemongrass #607— approx 900 yards/822 m of worsted weight yarn ④ MEDIUM

- Crochet hook: 6 mm (size J-10 U.S.) or size to obtain gauge
- Yarn needle

Gauge:
10 dc and 6 rows = 4 inches/10 cm
Always take time to check your gauge.

Stitches:
chain (ch)
double crochet (dc)

Notes:

1. Blanket is worked with 2 strands of yarn held together.
2. To change color, work last stitch of old color to last yarn over, yarn over with new color, and draw through all loops on hook to complete stitch. Proceed with new color. Fasten off old color.

INSTRUCTIONS

With 2 strands of A held together, ch 58.
Row 1: Dc in 4th ch from hook (beg ch does not count as a st) and in each chain across—55 dc.
Rows 2–4: Ch 3 (counts as first dc), turn, dc in each dc across.
Change to B in last dc of row 4.
Rows 5–34: Rep last row 30 more times, and change color as in the following stripe sequence:
Work 2 rows with B, 3 rows with C, 1 row with A, 4 rows with B, 2 rows with C, 3 rows with A, 1 row with B, 4 rows with C, 2 rows with A, 3 rows with B, 1 row with C, and 4 rows with A.
Fasten off.

FINISHING:
Weave in ends.

Circle Square Blanket

Design by Shara Chapek

Skill Level: Easy

Finished Measurements:
About 34 x 44½ inches/86.5 x 113 cm

Materials & Tools:
Lion Brand Vanna's Choice (100% acrylic; 3.5 ounces/100 g =170 yards/156 m):
(A), 4 balls, color white #100; (B), 1 ball, color dusty rose #140; (C), 1 ball, color pink #101; (D), 1 ball, color mustard #158; (E), 1 ball, color beige #123; (F), 1 ball, color goldfish #132; (G), 1 ball, color linen #099—approx 1700 yards/1560 m worsted weight yarn

- **Crochet hook:** 6 mm (size J-10 U.S) or size to obtain gauge
- Yarn Needle

Gauge:
One granny square measures about 5¼ inches/13.5 cm square.
Always take time to check your gauge.

Stitches:
chain (ch)
double crochet (dc)
slip stitch (sl st)
half double crochet (hdc)
single crochet (sc)

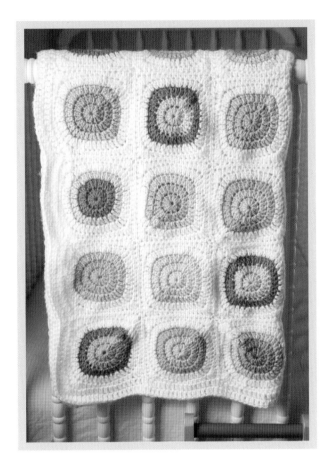

Notes:

1. Blanket is made from 48 granny squares. The first 3 rounds are worked in colors of your choice. The last 2 rounds should be worked using the main color (A).

2. Granny Squares are arranged into 8 rows of 6 squares each and then sewn together. A border is then worked around the entire outer edge of the blanket.

INSTRUCTIONS

GRANNY SQUARE (MAKE 48):

Rnd 1 (RS): With first color of your choice, ch 3, 12 dc in 3rd ch from hook (beg ch counts as first dc); join with sl st in top of beg ch—13 dc.

Rnd 2: Ch 2 (counts as first dc here and throughout), dc in same st as joining, 2 dc in each dc around; join with sl st in top of beg ch-2—26 dc. Fasten off.

Rnd 3: With RS facing, draw up a loop of 2nd color of your choice in same st as joining, ch 2, dc in same st as joining, [2 dc in next dc, dc in next dc] 12 times, sk last dc; join with sl st in top of beg ch-2—38 dc. Fasten off.

Rnd 4: With RS facing, draw up a loop of A (main color) in same st as joining, ch 2, [2 dc in next dc, dc in next 2 dc] 12 times, sk last dc; join with sl st in top of beg ch-2—49 dc.

Rnd 5: Ch 2, 3 dc in next dc (corner made), hdc in next 3 dc, sc in next 4 dc, hdc in next 4 dc, *4 dc in next dc (corner made), hdc in next 3 dc, sc in next 4 dc, hdc in next 4 dc; rep from * around; join with sl st in top of beg ch-2—60 sts. Fasten off.

FINISHING:

Arrange granny squares into a grid of 8 rows with 6 squares in each row. With A, sew squares together.

Border:

Rnd 1 (RS): With RS facing, draw up a loop of A in 2nd dc of any 4-dc corner, ch 2, 3 dc in same dc, *dc evenly spaced across edge to 2nd dc of next 4-dc corner, 4 dc in 2nd dc of corner; rep from * 2 more times, dc evenly spaced to end of rnd; join with sl st in top of beg ch 2.

Rnd 2: Ch 2, 4 dc in next dc (corner), dc evenly spaced across edge to 2nd dc of next 4-dc corner, 4 dc in next dc; rep from * 2 more times, dc evenly spaced to end of rnd; join with sl st in top of beg ch-2. Fasten off.

Weave in ends.

ABOUT THE DESIGNERS

SHEHNAAZ AFZAR is a designer with a passion for baby accessories. Her work has appeared on countless blogs, and she has been featured in *Simply Crochet* magazine. Shehnaaz loves crafting in all forms, be it sewing, knitting, painting, or embroidery, but crochet, by far, is her first love. Her future plans include developing an entire line of crochet baby accessories, and teaching crochet to children. You can find her crochet patterns at www. crochetdreamz.blogspot.com.

SARAH BAIN comes from a long line of needle artists and sees crocheting more as a sport than a hobby. After becoming a stay-at-home mom, this "sport" gave her a creative outlet to produce and sell her goods. Sarah's Etsy shop (SarahBain) features her original patterns in blankets, cowls, and accessories for the young and young at heart. When she's not working on items for her shop, she spends time with friends and family, including her husband and two sons.

JULIE BARBER is the artist and designer behind Blue J Crochet. She spends most of her time working as an Animal Services Officer in Southwest Michigan, where she resides with her husband, two boys, and a pack of rescued animals. Julie is inspired by bright, girly colors and all things sparkly, but being blessed with two boys has given her the ability to appreciate trains, cars, and tractors, too! Juggling work, school, and family has limited her crochet and crafts to nap time or after the kids' bedtime, which is the perfect way to unwind after a long and busy day.

MELINDA BROWN is the designer and creator of ClamTown, a unique collection of brightly-colored handmade items for adults, children, and the home. Her love of crafting and crocheting was influenced at a young age by her grandmother, and led her down a path to earning a degree in costuming for theater. Melinda works for the Los Angeles Opera by day and creates fun items inspired by the many special people in her life by night.

SHARA CHAPEK is originally from Alberta, Canada, and currently lives in Florida with her husband, Matt. Shara started crocheting and knitting a few years ago and hasn't looked back! She hopes to continue creating handmade items for babies and adults using beautiful yarns for the rest of her life. Her handmade creations can be found on Etsy at her shop, Ivory and Wool. Along with her husband, Shara is a missionary and works with youth all over the world.

ILARIA CHIARATTI has boundless energy and enthusiasm for crochet, interior décor, photograpy, and life. The Italian-born creative is based in the Netherlands and the owner of IDA Interior LifeStyle. Ilaria works as a freelance photographer for a number of publications and launched her blog in 2010. Her crochet creations are available on Etsy (www.etsy.com/shop/idalifestyle); she sells yarn at www.idayarnshop.com and blogs at www. idainteriorlifestyle.com. When she's not crocheting or working, she photographs, practices yoga, and organizes Italian dinners for her friends.

REBEKAH DESLOGE is a DIY kind of girl. Armed with a crochet hook and homemade T-shirt yarn, she creates an array of fun goods for kids, moms, and trendy ladies. Coming from a big family, Rebekah is constantly working to stand out from the pack and be unique. Her adventures in designing one-of-a-kind, eco-friendly crochet goods started when she had her first child, and she is now the proud mother of three beautiful children. You can find Rebekah's lovely, colorful crochet goods on etsy.com.shop/yourmomdesigns or on yourmomdesigns.com.

SIERRA GALLAGHER first learned to crochet when she was five years old, and she's been "hooked" ever since. Having worked in fashion, interior design, and as a hair stylist, coordinating texture and color comes easily to her. Sierra enjoys contrasting the traditional look of crochet with current trends, to create a modern aesthetic with a nostalgic feel. With her son as a model and muse, she started her own brand of modern handmade accessories. Check out her shop Fox + Rebel (www.foxandrebel.com) for new explorations and fresh accessories for every season.

SHANNON GILBRIDE is the owner/designer behind Gillyweeds and a mother of seven children. She began crocheting in 2005 to make wool cloth diaper covers for her little ones, and Gillyweeds was born. When not taking care of her family, she volunteers at church, crochets, scrapbooks, and dyes yarn. She is indebted to her wonderful husband for putting up with stashes of yarn and paper throughout the house! Find Shannon's work on Etsy (www.gillyweeds.etsy.com), on Facebook, (www.facebook.com/gillyweeds), or on her blog, www.gillyweeds.blogspot.com.

SHANNON GRAUPMAN is a stay-at-home mom living in Minnesota with her husband and four young children. When her third child was born in 2012, she opened an online shop called Little Buttercup Baby, selling her crochet hats, photo props, blankets, baby garments, nursing pads, and more! She inherited the "craft gene" from her Mom and made her first pair of mittens at age 12. You can find her work at www.littlebuttercupbaby.com and at www.facebook.com/littlebuttercupbabies.

KARA GUNZA is crochet blogger, designer, and instructor. Her blog, Petals to Picots (http://www.petalstopicots.com), is a celebration of crochet and other fiber arts. It is filled with helpful information and tutorials, gorgeous photography and inspiration, and boasts over 75 free crochet patterns (and counting!). Kara first learned to crochet when she was 9 years old from her grandmother. She now has more than 30 years crochet experience and recently graduated from the CGOA Masters of Advanced Stitches & Techniques program. Kara's designs can also be found in her shops on Etsy, Craftsy, Ravelry, and in her blog eShop. When Kara is not designing or teaching classes at her local yarn store, she is taking care of her husband and three children and their New Jersey home.

ANNEMARIE HAAKBLOG lives in the lovely city of Delft in The Netherlands with her boyfriend and an adopted stray cat from Spain. She took her first crochet class in 2010 and immediately fell in love with it, eventually designing her own patterns. Annemarie has published two crochet books in The Netherlands, and her patterns have been published on numerous websites and in international crochet magazines including Simply Crochet in the UK. You can find her designs at www.annemarieshaakblog. blogspot.com and in her Etsy shop at www.etsy.com /shop/annemariesbreiblog.

JENNIFER HALVORSON is originally from Montana but lives in Portland, Oregon with her yarn-weary-but-understanding husband, Brennan, and their adorable and hilarious son, Torvie. She started crocheting about eight years ago, and quickly became obsessed! That obsession blossomed into a business with her Etsy shop, Fritz & Tootie (www.etsy.com/shop/fritzandtootie), where she peddles her whimsical wares for children. When not crocheting, Jennifer enjoys embroidery, needle felting, reading, documentaries, gardening, canning, playing board games, and spending time with her family.

EMMA LAMB is a British girl living in the beautiful city of Edinburgh, Scotland. She is a blogger, textile designer, crocheter, and online shop owner. Emma has appeared as an Etsy Featured Seller, and her work has been featured in UK Handmade Magazine. With an eye for detail and an uncompromising standard for quality, she creates designs that are practical as well as beautiful works of art. Her current collection explores fresh and playful combinations of color, pattern, and texture with a nod to retro styles. Emma draws inspiration from the Scandinavian aesthetic, mid-century design, and her everyday life. See more at www.etsy.com/shop/EmmaLamb.

KRISTEN LEITNER is the owner of Snowfall Studio, an online shop that sells hand-crocheted toys. Her love of crochet began at age 12 when she bought a book to teach herself the craft. Today, Kristen's patterns are inspired by her four children and their love of animals. As an artisan and mom, Kristen is committed to using eco-friendly natural fibers to create unique toys for kids. She has designed patterns for flamingos, hedgehogs, sea turtles, jellyfish, sheep, cats, owls, and more. With Snowfall Studio's soft toys, it's all about the cuteness factor! Visit her Etsy shop at www.etsy.com/shop/SnowFallStudio.

HEATHER MAIN opened her Etsy shop (www.onheathershook.etsy.com) in 2010 after the birth of her son. She loves to work with bright colors and create handmade items for families to cherish. Heather is in school for nursing but still manages to find time to relax on the waters of eastern North Carolina. Swimming off of a sandbar, fishing for dinner, and camping right on the boat mean that once in a while her yarn or textbooks end up a little sandy, but she thinks life is much better with a little sunshine and saltwater.

LENKA MOORE, from Prague, Czech Republic, learned to crochet as a child from her mother. She studied dance when she was younger and grew up surrounded by music and the arts. Lenka moved to the United States when she was 20 years old. She sells her crochet goods in her Etsy shop, Shy Lemon. Lenka also enjoys knitting and painting and recently started taking sewing classes, though crochet is by far her biggest passion.

CAMILLE JACKS MORGAN is originally from Jamaica. She attended the Savannah College of Art and Design on a portfolio scholarship and earned a BFA in computer art and animation in 1996. After having her daughter, she gave up painting and drawing but eventually taught herself how to crochet. Camille has published her patterns in several magazines, and she's been twice featured in *Home and Garden DIY* magazine. Her doily rugs have been sold in more than 12 countries.

ROSEMARY NEWMAN is one of those lucky people who comes from a long line of makers. She learned to crochet, knit, sew, and quilt at a young age, and the love for all things fiber and fabric has stuck. Today, she's lucky enough to be able to earn a living as a maker. Rosie currently designs and creates cute, colorful kids' toys under her brand name, rosieok, on Etsy. She splits her time between crocheting cute toys, handspinning, and dyeing snuggly yarns.

BRIANA OLSEN designs crochet patterns from her home in Utah. She particularly loves designing loveys and hats with unique stitches and interesting textures. Briana is married and is a stay-at-home mom with one son, whom she frequently uses to model her projects. She attended to Brigham Young University, where her love of learning led her to elementary education. In her spare time (when she isn't crocheting), she can be found reading, playing with her family, or learning yet another hobby.

DEBBIE RONEY started crocheting and knitting at the tender age of 9, when her mother instilled in her a love for needle arts. Now, at 62, she's still at it! With her family's encouragement, she opened an Etsy shop, Grizzly Creek, and has been happily crafting anything that crosses her path and sharing it in her shop. Debbie lives and crafts in northern California with her husband, and believes that life's too short not to play.

LORI JO SHOEMAKE has more than 30 years of self-taught experience in crocheting, knitting, sewing, machine embroidery, sketch work, and rubberstamping, and she considers her work a heart and hands tribute to the memories of her Grandma Jo. Lori Jo lives in the Atlanta, Georgia, area with her husband, their little Pekingese, "Lily," and two beautiful college-age daughters. She sells her handmade hats, sweaters, and custom work in her Etsy shop, The Preppy Peach Boutique (www.preppypeach.etsy.com).

IMGE TEKUZ is the mother of two lovely girls who inspire her every day. She loves using unexpected color combinations to create unique designs for little ones and enjoys adding fun details with yarns, ribbons, and buttons. For the best results, she sources the best materials for each and every one of the accessories she makes. Imge thinks there's the perfect hat for every child, and she strives to create designs that are fun for kids to wear and that look great too. For winter accessories visit her Etsy shop My Baby Hats (www.etsy.com/shop/mybabyhats), and browse her selection of yarn at CottonNmore (www.etsy.com/shop/cottonnmore).

CLARE TROWBRIDGE is a homemaker and educator to her three young children in rural West Sussex, England. Much of the inspiration behind the patterns and kits she sells grow out of her own family's needs. Her business also reflects her family's long-standing commitment to making sustainable choices in both the big things and the little things in life. Her ready-made items use planet-friendly and ethically-sourced fibers, and her patterns often involve upcycling secondhand materials. See more at www.littleconkers.co.uk.

MAAIKE VAN KOERT draws inspiration from her daily life and surroundings in a little village in the south of The Netherlands, where she lives with her husband, Jeroen, and chocolate Lab, Floyd. A creative woman at heart, Maaike is always working on several projects. After paper, origami, painting, and drawing, it was only a matter of time before she would discover yarn and start designing with it. Maaike's designs are all about the right amount and mix of color. See more at www.etsy.com/shop/creJJtion and visit her blog, www.creJJtion.com, for more inspiration and craft ideas.

ABOUT THE AUTHOR

KATHLEEN MCCAFFERTY is a crafty dabbler with a love for color, crochet, and all things cute. She is the editor of several Lark titles including *The Collage Workbook, Making Handmade Books, PUSH Paper,* and *PUSH Print,* and the author of *Making Mini Books* and *Craft-In.* She lives life to the fullest in beautiful Asheville, North Carolina, with Ira G., her scruffy terrier, always at her side.

ACKNOWLEDGMENTS

My gratitude goes out to the fabulous Lark Books editor, Amanda Carestio, for giving me the opportunity to bring *Baby Brights* into the world, and to her sweet little daughter Ruby, for providing crafty inspiration and the need for a fresh new book with baby crochet items! Beth Sweet, Lark Books' editor extraordinaire, worked closely to help me develop the project list with her usual enthusiasm and impeccable taste, and championed the book from the start. Editor Jill Jarnow at Sterling helped me bring the book into the home stretch, pinning down the last details and shepherding it along so that it's the lovely book you now hold in your hands. This book wouldn't have been possible without the amazing designers that contributed their projects, patterns, and their time. I appreciate each and every one of you! Finally, I'd like to thank my mom, Eilish McCafferty, to whom I dedicate this book, for showing me a world filled with color, brightness, and crafty goodness. I love you.

INDEX

Note: Page numbers in *italics* indicate projects. Page numbers in **bold** indicate designer information.